The Responsible Public Servant

D0965011

The Responsible Public Servant

by

Kenneth Kernaghan

and

John W. Langford

The Institute for Research on Public Policy/
L'Institut de recherches politiques

The Institute of Public Administration of Canada/
L'Institut d'administration publique du Canada

Printed in Canada

Legal Deposit First Quarter
Bibliothéque nationals du Québec

Canadian Cataloguing in Publication Data

Kernaghan, Kenneth, 1940–

The responsible public servant

Co-published by the
Institute of Public Administration of Canada.
Prefatory material in English and French.
Includes bibliographical references.
ISBN 0-88645-099-3

1. Canada–Officials and employees–Professional ethics.
2. Civil service ethics–Canada.
3. Public administration–Moral and ethical aspects.
4. Public administration–Canada.
I. Langford, John W. II. Institute for Research on Public Policy.
III. Institute of Public Administration of Canada.
IV. Title.

JL108.K57 1990   172'.2   C90-097547-4

Published by
The Institute for Research on Public Policy
L'Institut de recherches politiques
1470, rue Peel, Suite 200
Montréal (Québec) H3A 1T1

For Helgi and Kate

Contents

Foreword

For the Institute for Research on Public Policy, this book represents a key element in a program of work focussing on the convulsive forces affecting the management of the public sector in Canada. Earlier publications on this subject include *Implosion* and *Ou aller?*, by Nicole S. Morgan, *Beyond the Bottom Line*, by Timothy Plumptre, and *The Vertical Solitude*, by David Zussman and Jak Jabes.

This book continues that discussion of issues in public management. It and the eight one-hour video programs (also entitled *The Responsible Public Servant*) which the Institute for Research on Public Policy co-produced with the University of Victoria in 1988 confront the ethical dilemmas resulting from collapse of the long-established consensus within the public services of Canada about how appointed public officials should behave. The book and the videos explore the key areas in which public servants are struggling to re-establish some consensus on values and ethical principles to guide their relationships with their political masters, clients and colleagues. They ask the question: What does it mean, in the last decade of the 20th century, for a public servant to act responsibly?

As is inevitable in a project designed to focus on the values driving a rapidly evolving organizational culture, this book and the accompanying video series ask more questions than they answer. Public servants are bound by written rules and conventions in a number of the areas discussed (e.g. political neutrality, confidentiality, conflict of interest), but in most jurisdictions in Canada and many other democratic countries long-standing rules and conventions of conduct are being questioned and discarded. In any case, such rules and conventions are not consistent from one jurisdiction to another. What is viewed as perfectly appropriate behaviour in the public service of one government can be seen as completely unacceptable in another. By contrast, some of the values explored are hardly mentioned in the statements and literature which form the foundation for public sector organizational cultures. The duty to protect the privacy of citizens and the obligation to serve the public, for instance, remain fuzzy, formless commandments for most public servants.

As part of its own commitment to advocating the values and ideals of public service and encouraging the highest standards of professional practice, the Institute of Public Administration of Canada has also long been interested in public service ethics. In 1974 it commissioned, and later published, a study entitled *Ethical Conduct: Guidelines for Government Employees* by Kenneth Kernaghan. In 1986 the Institute, after extensive consultation with its members, adopted **"The Statement of Principles Regarding the Conduct of Public Servants."** This new work by Kernaghan and Langford complements the IPAC "Statement."

The Institute of Public Administration of Canada is pleased to make yet another contribution to the literature on public service ethics by joining with the Institute for Research on Public Policy to support this publication, *The Responsible Public Servant.*

It is our hope that this book and video series will help public servants think through and reformulate the rules by which they live their professional lives. The absence of consensus on the nature of good conduct is an important problem of public policy. However, as Kernaghan and Langford argue persuasively, it is not one which will be solved by new codes of conduct dictated and imposed from above. With the wise counsel of their senior managers and political masters, public servants have to work out for themselves what behaviour is appropriate. In the end, whatever the regimes of accountability or scrutiny, it can only be their own conscience that provides their guide.

Pierre E. Coulombe
President
Institute of Public
  Administration of Canada

Rod Dobell
President
Institute for Research
  on Public Policy

Avant-propos

Pour l'Institut de recherches politiques, cet ouvrage constitue une étape importante dans un programme de travail centré sur l'étude des forces désordonnées auxquelles se trouve livrée la gestion du secteur public au Canada. Dans le même ordre de préoccupations, plusieurs études ont déjà paru, dont : *Implosion* et *Où aller?*, de Nicole S. Morgan, *Beyond the Bottom Line*, de Timothy Plumptre et *The Vertical Solitude* de David Zussman et Jak Jabes.

Le présent ouvrage, de même que la série de huit programmes vidéo d'une heure chacun portant le même titre (*The Responsible Public Servant*, "Le fonctionnaire responsable"), continuent le débat que l'IRP a publié en collaboration avec l'Université de Victoria, en 1988. Le livre et les programmes vidéo s'attaquent aux problèmes d'éthique suscités par la disparition du consensus qui, établi depuis longtemps, régit les normes de comportement des fonctionnaires nommés au sein de la fonction publique. Y sont passés en revue les principaux secteurs qui font l'objet d'une réflexion sérieuse de la part des fonctionnaires dans le but de rétablir un consensus sur les valeurs et les principes d'éthique qui devraient les guider dans leurs rapports avec leurs patrons politiques, le public et leurs collègues. On y pose la question suivante : que signifie agir d'une manière responsable pour le fonctionnaire de la dernière décennie du 20ème siècle?

Comme on pouvait s'y attendre d'un tel projet visant à expliquer les valeurs d'une structure en pleine évolution, ce livre, ainsi que la série de vidéos qui l'accompagne, soulèvent beaucoup plus de questions qu'ils n'en résolvent. Les fonctionnaires sont liés par des règlements et des usages conventionnels dans bien des domaines parmi ceux qui sont évoqués (par exemple, en matière de neutralité politique, de secret professionnel et de conflit d'intérêts). Pourtant, ces règlements et usages établis de longue date sont partout remis en question, aussi bien dans la fonction publique canadienne que dans celle de nombreux autres pays démocratiques. Qui plus est, ces règlements et usages conventionnels varient selon les juridictions : ce qui est considéré comme parfaitement approprié dans l'une peut être jugé totalement inacceptable dans une autre. Par contre, certaines des valeurs examinées ici sont à peine mentionnées dans les déclarations et les écrits qui se trouvent à la base des principes organisationnels du secteur public. Le devoir de protéger la vie privée des citoyens, par exemple, ainsi que l'obligation de servir le public, demeurent des principes vagues et sans application pratique pour la plupart des fonctionnaires.

Dans le cadre de sa mission visant à promouvoir les valeurs et les idéaux dans la fonction publique et à encourager l'excellence des normes dans la pratique professionnelle, l'Institut d'administration publique du Canada s'intéresse aussi depuis longtemps aux questions d'éthique dans la fonction publique. En 1974, il a commissionné et par la suite publié une étude de Kenneth Kernaghan, intitulée *Comportement professionnel : directives à l'intention des fonctionnaires*. Puis en 1986, après consultation avec ses membres, l'Institut adoptait "La déclaration de principes relative à la conduite des fonctionnaires". Ce nouveau livre de M. Kernaghan et Langford, vient compléter la "déclaration" de l'IAPC.

Aussi l'Institut d'administration publique est-il heureux de pouvoir contribuer une fois de plus aux études consacrées à l'éthique de la fonction publique en joignant ses efforts à ceux de l'Institut de recherches politiques pour la publication de *The Responsible Public Servant*.

Nous espérons que cet ouvrage et la série de vidéos aideront les fonctionnaires à repenser et à reformuler les règles qui régissent leur vie professionnelle. L'absence de consensus sur ce sujet est un problème de politique générale important. Pourtant, comme le montrent d'une manière convaincante Messieurs Kernaghan et Langford, cette question ne se résoudra pas grâce à des codes d'éthique qui leur seront imposés par leurs supérieurs. C'est aux fonctionnaires eux-mêmes de décider de la conduite la plus appropriée, en suivant les sages conseils de leurs cadres supérieurs et ceux de leurs dirigeants politiques. En fin de compte, quels que soient les modalités et le régime de contrôle selon lesquels ils doivent rendre compte, c'est à leur propre conscience qu'ils devront demander de les éclairer.

Pierre E. Coulombe
Président
Institut d'administration publique
  du Canada

Rod Dobell
Président
Institut de recherches
  politiques

Acknowledgments

This book is the result of the happy coincidence of two events, each involving one of the book's authors. In 1984 Ken Kernaghan began work for the Institute of Public Administration of Canada on a Statement of Principles, an article on the Statement for the Institute's journal, and a book on how Canada's public employees should behave. A year later John Langford began work on a project co-sponsored by the University of Victoria and the Institute for Research on Public Policy (IRPP) to develop a video package on the theme of the responsible public servant. A book to accompany the video package was begun shortly after, while John Langford was a fellow-in-residence at IRPP. In 1986 the two book projects were combined.

As usual with projects of this sort, many people deserve notice for their assistance. In addition to the intellectual debt to one another and the anonymous reviewers of the manuscript, each author has his own list of acknowledgments. Starting in Victoria, John Langford owes a special vote of thanks to Ken Huffman for his research assistance with both the book and the video series. Most of the cases in the book were put into dialogue form by Janice Carlson. Both the cases and the draft manuscript were refined after repeated exposure to the MPA ethics course at the University of Victoria. Several colleagues and friends read draft chapters. They include Eike-Henner Kluge, Warren Langford, Brian Marson, Dick Noble, Steven Owen, and Murray Rankin. The IRPP and, in particular, Rod Dobell, Lorne Brownsey, and Steve Rosell were unfailingly supportive of both the book and the video projects. Marion Voelkel designed the book cover. Sheila Fuller and Wendy Shergold smoothed out my "word perfect" copy. Finally, Kate Seaborne, in a professional capacity, was a key participant in the preparation of the video series and the development of the structure of the book. As the ultimate measure of her personal support, she actually married John Langford in late 1987. It is for this and so much more that this book is in part dedicated to her.

This book is also dedicated to Ken Kernaghan's wife, Helgi, who for more than 25 years has endured his fascination with public administration in general and administrative ethics in particular. In addition, Ken acknowledges the enormous debt owed to public servants, academic colleagues, and students who have helped him to refine his ideas on administrative responsibility, values, and ethics. Many of these ideas have been examined critically in government workshops, at scholarly conferences, and in his university courses. Finally, deep appreciation is extended to the Institute of Public Administration of Canada. The Institute published Ken's first book on public service ethics and many of its members provided extremely helpful assistance with the drafting of the Statement of Principles Regarding the Conduct of Public Employees which provided part of the impetus for the writing of this book.

Introduction

Is it acceptable for a public servant to blow the whistle? Should a public servant be able to moonlight? Should public servants feel obligated to forgo their political rights? To what levels of risk should public servants expose members of the public? Answers to questions such as these won't be found in this book; we try hard not to be prescriptive about what is good or bad. What this book does provide is a practical examination of the arguments that are made on both – or many – sides of these and other difficult value questions currently confronting public servants.[1] Thinking about these questions won't make decisions any easier, but it should cause public sector managers (or prospective public sector managers) to reflect on how they currently deal with ethical dilemmas in their public lives and may even provoke them to approach some of these problems differently.

It is our firm conviction that public servants and those who educate and train them have for too long ignored the ethical dimension of public sector management. Schools of public administration and government training programs prepare public servants for the technical challenges that they confront as managers, but traditionally have left them largely unequipped to deal with what Mark Pastin refers to as the "hard problems of management."[2] In our view, nothing is more dangerous than a public servant who is technically fit but ethically flabby. Public servants and their masters must accept that much of their work involves difficult value choices. They must accept responsibility for the hard choices, and learn how to think ethically and justify their decisions. The most subversive purpose of this book is to introduce a habit of ethical discourse into the conduct of public affairs; to make moral calculus as important as the quantitative analysis of policy options or the efficient management of financial resources.

What is the Book About?

What are the big value questions facing appointed officials? What issues do we focus on in this book? In general terms, we are concerned about how an individual public servant should act when he or she is involved in activities of government that affect members of the public, fellow employees, political and administrative superiors, and the society as a whole. We are interested in provoking thought and discussion about the nature of obligations and duties, the balancing of conflicting values, and the goodness and badness of administrative practices and public policies. Obviously, in our view, there is more to being ethical than the mere avoidance of corruption.

This study examines the traditional and current meanings of the primary principles or "commandments" to which the responsible public servant is expected to adhere. These commandments are: act in the public interest; be politically neutral; do not disclose confidential information; protect the privacy of citizens and employees; provide efficient, effective and fair service to the public; avoid conflicts of interest; and be accountable.

Chapter 1 begins by explaining why there is so much uncertainty as to what constitutes responsible bureaucratic behaviour and how this uncertainty came about. Arguments that public servants need not, or should not, concern themselves with ethical and value issues are rejected on the basis of a critical analysis of the "ethic of neutrality," the "ethic of structure," the notion of ethical relativism, and the view that there can be no difference between public and private morality. Then attention is focused on the central question of how public servants do, and should, go about making and justifying their ethical choices. Special consideration is given to the utilitarian and deontological approaches to ethical justification, with particular reference to the public sector. Frequent reference to these two approaches is made throughout the book.

The concept of the public interest, which is discussed in chapter 2, is closely linked to the examination of responsible bureaucratic behaviour in chapter 1. Indeed, the public servant's duty to act in the public interest is very similar in meaning to the broad duty to "act responsibly." Chapter 2 is based on the conclusion that the public interest is a credible and useful concept. With a view to explaining how the public interest can be used as an operational guide, four major approaches to decision-making in the public interest are outlined. These are the dominant-value, procedural, consensualist, and cost-benefit approaches. In addition to these approaches, each of which is derived directly from theoretical writings on the public interest, two other important considerations are examined. First is the argument that by devotion to "neutral service" public servants can avoid concern about the public interest. Second is the importance of public servants avoiding self-interest in favour of the public interest. The conclusion is drawn in this chapter that no one theoretical approach has been universally accepted as the best possible guide to decision-making in the public interest. Yet certain insights drawn from each approach provide the responsible public servant with practical guidelines for such decision-making.

Chapter 3 examines the duty of the public servant to adhere to the constitutional convention of political neutrality. This duty to be politically neutral is broken down into several more specific duties, each of which is discussed separately. These duties are: appoint and promote only on the basis of merit; be non-partisan; avoid public comment on government policies; preserve your anonymity; and be loyal. These duties are interpreted differently from one government to another and even within a single government. Moreover, in light of changes in relations among public servants, politicians, and the public, there is considerable disagreement as to whether some of these duties are realistic in contemporary governments. This chapter examines the integral links between political neutrality and the constitutional conventions of ministerial responsibility and public service anonymity. The conclusion is drawn that the meaning of the public servant's duty to be politically neutral is in a state of flux.

Chapter 4 deals with the two interrelated issues of confidentiality and privacy. In respect of confidentiality, it is notable that the public servant's duty to keep certain information confidential clashes with a duty to satisfy the commitment of politicians to "open government" and to meet the disclosure requirements of freedom of information legislation. Despite the many rules providing direction as to what information public servants can or cannot disclose, there is considerable uncertainty as to how the responsible public servant should act in this sphere. This chapter reviews the arguments for and against secrecy and assesses the practices of deception, disinformation, propaganda, and censorship. Particular attention is paid to the ethical dilemma of whistle-blowing.

Protection of the privacy of individual and corporate citizens and or other governments is one of the primary justifications for confidentiality. But consideration of the public servant's duty of privacy requires an examination of what kinds of information governments should be collecting and what constraints should be placed on the means by which it is collected and on the purposes for which it is used. The tendency of many public servants to violate principles of fair information practice in the face of contending values is noted. The responsible public servant must balance carefully the protection of privacy against such other values as open government, and efficiency and effectiveness in service to the public.

The public servant's duty of service to the public is examined in chapter 5. Two major justifications are offered for this duty: the responsibility to the public required of government officials in our liberal democratic society; and the obligation to serve the public so as to preserve and enhance the dignity of other human beings. Among the key values involved in the duty of service to the public are responsiveness, efficiency, effectiveness, and fairness. The challenge for the responsible public servant is that these values can both complement and clash with one another. Moreover, their meaning is interpreted in different ways by the public, politicians, and public servants. The fact that there are, for example, varying interpretations of the value of fairness is especially problematic in light of the increasing importance attached to procedural fairness in public administration. It is argued that the general duty of service to the public needs to be instilled more securely in the organizational culture of the public service.

Difficult issues of interpretation arise also in the examination of conflict of interest in chapter 6. The public servant's duty to avoid conflicts of interest is complicated by several factors. First, the definition of what constitutes a conflict has been significantly broadened in recent years. Public servants are enjoined to avoid not only real conflicts, but apparent and potential conflicts as well. Secondly, there are many variations of conflict of interest, including, for example, influence-peddling, moonlighting, and accepting benefits. Thirdly, the nature, extent, and application of conflict of interest rules vary from one government, even one department, to another. Fourthly, the discretionary power of public servants, combined with the vast size and complexity of government, gives them many opportunities to use public office for private gain. Finally, the public and the media are less tolerant of conflicts of interest involving public officials. Increasing attention needs to be directed to ensuring that rules designed to deter and punish conflicts of interest do not encroach unduly on the rights of responsible public servants.

Chapter 7 is concerned with the public servant's duty to be accountable for his or her decisions and recommendations. The accountability of public servants is one of the major issues of contemporary governance. A distinction is made between the terms responsibility and accountability, but it is acknowledged that in popular discussions the terms are often used interchangeably. It is acknowledged also that the traditional meaning of bureaucratic accountability has been considerably broadened. To deal adequately with the duty of accountability, it is necessary to consider the questions: Accountability to whom? for what? by what means? Many public servants are uncertain about the correct answers to these questions. This uncertainty is exacerbated by the fact that the value of accountability frequently clashes with such other values as responsiveness, efficiency, and effectiveness.

The final chapter considers what institutional means and techniques can be used to strengthen and encourage responsible public service. Here the emphasis shifts from an exploration of what constitutes good or responsible behaviour to an examination of the steps which managers can take to make responsible administrative behaviour part of the organizational culture of government. In focusing on the institutional setting within which public servants operate, we subscribe fully to Kathryn Denhardt's thesis that "the organizational context and the individual development of the administrator must *both* be integral parts of any approach to administrative ethics."[3]

Within the commandments examined in chapters 2 through 7 are embedded most of the "on-the-job" value dilemmas which contemporary public servants confront. The problem is that these commandments as interpreted within federal, provincial, and municipal jurisdictions across the country do not provide public servants with uniform and clear messages about how they should handle such dilemmas. Or, where rules are stated relatively clearly, they are often seen to be inappropriate, anachronistic, or indefensible. There is no longer a widely shared consensus about what it means to be a responsible public servant. The orthodox religion of responsible behaviour is constantly under attack or simply declared to be irrelevant. In short, the "seven commandments" are suffering from a credibility gap.

As a result, public servants are confronted with a bewildering array of competing edicts, practices, and pressures. Should I be loyal or politically neutral? Should I be open and accessible to the public or maximize my efficiency? Is the effectiveness of the program more important than the privacy of its clients? Am I accountable only upward to the minister or horizontally to my colleagues and downward to the client groups of my department? Can I help to build a new conservative social policy after a decade of involvement in the construction of the welfare state?[4]

Our concern, then, is to see what sense can be made of these seven commandments in the context of the often harsh contemporary world of choices which public servants face. We will be trying to strip away the rhetoric to examine the justification of positions for and against these rules and the actions they seem to dictate in specific situations.

Using this Book

In draft form, this book has been used successfully by the authors in both undergraduate and graduate courses devoted exclusively or in part to ethical problems in public administration. Individual chapters have also been employed equally successfully as background reading for management training seminars on specific subjects. The book has been intentionally pitched at the middle management level in an effort to avoid the dangerous tendency, rampant in Canadian writing about public administration, to assume that all the readers are likely to be deputy ministers.

Each chapter contains cases which have also been field tested successfully in the classroom. Obviously, these cases do not begin to exhaust the variety of dilemmas which public servants confront as they go about their day-to-day work. Our experience suggests that students and management course participants are only too willing to provide case material from their own experience. While short, "snapshot" case scenarios can provoke the practical exchanges that make the discussion of value dilemmas come to life, they usually suffer from one serious drawback. They rarely give the student an accurate feel for the time frame over which public servants get pulled into more and more difficult dilemmas by the accretion of seemingly small and unimportant decisions or actions.

The contents of this book were designed to complement the study of the Institute of Public Administration of Canada's Statement of Principles (see Appendix). The Statement was developed by the Institute as part of its commitment "to promote and maintain high ideals and traditions in the public service," and "to give expression to the considered view of the members on questions of public duty." In addition, the Statement is intended to advance the profession of public administration in Canada; to enhance the public's image of public service; to inform the public, politicians, and the news media of the principles which should guide the behaviour of appointed officials; and to deal with issues (for example, political rights) arising from guarantee of fundamental freedoms contained in the Canadian Charter of Human Rights and Freedoms. This book devotes a chapter or a substantial part of a chapter to each of the major sections of the Statement.[5]

The book is also designed as an accompanying text for a series of eight one-hour videos entitled "The Responsible Public Servant," prepared jointly by the University of Victoria and the Institute for Research on Public Policy. These videotapes contain not only expert analysis of the subject matter of each of the eight chapters, but also role plays of most of the cases in the book and analysis of these cases by practising public servants.[6]

Notes

1. While many of the problems addressed in this book are shared by elected as well as appointed public officials, our primary focus throughout is on the latter.

2. Mark Pastin, *The Hard Problems of Management* (San Francisco: Jossey-Bass, 1986).

3. Kathryn G. Denhardt, *The Ethics of Public Service: Resolving Moral Dilemmas in Public Organizations* (New York: Greenwood Press, 1988), p. 3.

4. These questions are explored in more detail in John W. Langford, "Responsibility in the Senior Public Service: Marching to Several Drummers" *Canadian Public Administration* 27 (Winter, 1984), pp. 513-21.

5. Copies of the IPAC "Statement of Principles" can be obtained by writing to the Institute of Public Administration of Canada, 897 Bay Street, Toronto, M5S 1Z7, Ontario.

6. Information concerning the purchase of the "Responsible Public Servant" video series can be obtained by writing to the Program Coordinator, Public Administration, Division of University Extension, University of Victoria, Victoria, B.C., V8W 2Y2.

Chapter 1

Thinking about Responsible Behaviour

Before examining the key commandments or rules to which Canadian public servants are generally asked to adhere, we have some underbrush to clear and foundations to lay. This chapter first tries to sort out why the ethical world of public servants is so confusing. Why isn't the nature of good behaviour obvious? How did this uncertainty about the nature of responsible administrative behaviour emerge? We then go on to tackle a number of questions which are often used to deny the necessity for public servants to think ethically. Is ethics really the concern of government managers? Aren't most public servants just bit players in a drama in which the real choices are made by administrative and political superiors or, alternatively, by so many people that no one individual is responsible for them? In any case, aren't ethical questions all relative? Why worry about justifying your behaviour if there is no possibility of determining what the right answer is? We then raise the question of the acceptability of ruthlessness in public life. Is public morality different from private morality? These issues lead us inevitably to the hardest question of all. Assuming that public servants must justify their ethical choices, how should this be done? The latter part of the chapter tries to provide the public servant with an ethical "tool kit," some techniques and theories for dealing with the hard questions.

Isn't Good Behaviour Obvious?

Why is there so little consensus today about what it means to be a responsible public servant? Why has the question of the morality of public officials become such a public issue? An easy answer to these related questions is that the media are to blame. There is no doubt that the media are providing the public with much more coverage of cases involving questionable behaviour on the part of elected and appointed officials. Investigative reporting and better access to government information allow the media to present detailed stories about the means, ends, and methods of modern governments and officials. These stories make good copy and interact nicely with what many commentators agree is a burgeoning loss of public confidence in governmental institutions.[1] Whatever their effect on public confidence, stories about such issues as conflict of interest, whistle-blowing, breakdowns in accountability, and struggles by public servants for political rights, leave an impression that there is turmoil among both elected and appointed public officials about what responsible public behaviour looks like. A few commentators argue that there is no evidence that behaviour in the public sector has become worse. However, more suggest – on the strength of cases featuring involvement by public servants in partisan political activities or serious violations of the privacy of citizens, for instance – that traditional standards have weakened and that Canada's reputation for a decent, reliable, and neutral public service is being eroded.

Increased media coverage of such events as the Watergate scandal in the United States and the Sinclair Stevens and Patricia Starr cases in Canada may partly explain our continuing fixation with the integrity of government officials. However, such coverage does not in itself provide an adequate explanation for the widespread questioning about what it means to be a responsible public servant. For such an explanation we have to look at changes within government and the public service, and to the evolving relationship between public servants and politicians.

Two factors most commonly seized upon are the size and role of the public service. It is argued that the growth in the public service from the Second World War into the 1970s (and for some provincial and municipal governments into the 1980s) was a deciding factor in the fragmentation of its organizational culture. What in virtually all jurisdictions in Canada had been tightly knit bands of public servants, led often by "kit-bag" mandarins with several years of military experience behind them, became big, anonymous bureaucratic units with large numbers of new, unsocialized recruits and a necessarily distant, inaccessible leadership group. That leadership was incapable of commanding the deference toward its values and rules that had been accorded to those of the mythologized mandarins. To make matters worse, many of the new public servants came from the private sector and professional groups, bringing with them diverse and often very different values and standards of conduct. To this complex brew was added the factor of unionization and its potential for the introduction of competing values and loyalties.

Throughout this period the traditional organizational culture was further undermined by subtle but important changes in the role of public servants. The increased scope and complexity of government's intervention in the economy and society meant that many decisions involving substantive policy were clearly being made by public servants. This trend has been reinforced more recently by the impact of private sector "managerial" thinking on public sector organizations. The effect has been to encourage the devolution of discretionary decision-making power on to lower and lower levels of management. As a result the traditional distinction between politics and administration is broken and public servants face new questions about the meaning of neutrality, how they go about deciding what policy, regulation, or decision is in the public interest, and to whom they should be accountable.

The explosion of public sector activity also brought new pressures on the public service culture from "guardian" organizations within government. Riding the mid-1970s wave of concern about the financial management practices of government, auditors general and comptrollers became powerful champions of the values of economy, efficiency, and effectiveness. Similarly, the courts and the new provincial ombudsmen entered the arena on behalf of the values of fairness and procedural equity. Freedom of information and privacy commissioners fostered openness on the one hand, and privacy on the other. Much of this may be old wine in new bottles, but it has had the effect of disturbing the hierarchy of traditional values and forcing the public servant to face squarely hard choices between values such as privacy and efficiency, effectiveness and fairness, and openness and confidentiality.

But the suggested disintegration of the traditional value system does not end here. Over the last decade the public sector administrative culture has been further disoriented by the neo-conservative counter-revolution which in most jurisdictions has taken the form of cutbacks and the contracting out of public services. The high premium placed on mobility and term employment has had the inevitable effect of reducing the possibility of building strong organizational cultures based on the notion of a "career" public service. This disintegrative phenomenon is enhanced in some jurisdictions by politicization of the managerial ranks of the public service and by the sense that a high premium is being placed on fairly simple-minded forms of loyalty to the "team." The traditional package of public service values did not contemplate a situation in which public servants would become little more than transient agents of their political masters.

Every reader will undoubtedly be able to note other factors that have contributed to the contemporary questioning of the meaning and relevance of the traditional statements of public service values. Some pressures seem obviously contradictory in their impact. For instance, forces inclined to decentralize authority and increase the decision-making independence of public servants would appear to be at odds with pressures designed to bind the public servant more tightly to the policy leadership of the political executive.[2] The more important point for this study, however, is that both pressures tend to destabilize the classic relationship between politicians and public servants, leaving the latter uncertain about what represents appropriate behaviour toward politicians, colleagues, clients, and citizens more generally.

Public Servants as Independent Moral Actors

One antidote to this confusion about how a responsible public servant should act is to avoid the issue altogether by arguing that public servants are not independent moral actors. The muddle of confusing and conflicting values confronting public servants then becomes irrelevant because the responsibility for value choices is diffused or transferred to the organization or to the elected officials they serve. These are important arguments and their limitations must be understood before we can proceed confidently on the assumption that public servants are individually responsible for government decisions and actions in which they are involved.

Dennis Thompson argues that an attempt to absolve the public servant of moral responsibility is really made up of two distinct theories, the ethic of neutrality and the ethic of structure. The former argues that:

> ... administrators are ethically neutral in the sense that they do not exercise independent moral judgment. They are not expected to act on any moral principles of their own, but are to give effect to whatever principles are reflected in the orders and policies they are charged with implementing ... Their aim should always be to discover what policy other people (usually elected officials) intend or would intend; or in the case of conflicting directives to interpret legally or constitutionally who has the authority to determine policy ... The ethic of neutrality portrays the ideal administrator as a completely reliable instrument of the goals of the organization, never injecting personal values into the process of furthering these goals.[3]

Under this model, public servants may be permitted to dispute the logic of their leadership up to the point of decision, but when the views of the top officials are known, public servants must fall in line or resign.

One significant problem with this approach is that it does not reflect the reality of modern public administration. Public servants are not robots. All the evidence indicates that they often work in a leadership vacuum in which they initiate policy, develop support for it, and are held to account for their role by political leaders and the affected members of the public.

Another flaw in the neutrality argument is the unrealistically narrow set of options which it offers the public servant. To insist that a public servant obey or resign places him or her in an impossible position, implying that to stay in office is to consent to the policy or practice in question. The ethic of neutrality would soon rid governments of all public servants except those who agree wholeheartedly and at all times with the government of the day. Such an approach suggests that there is no room for any form of dissent by public servants except resignation. Clearly, the wide range of arguments which we will examine on actions such as whistle-blowing and public comment suggests that an ethic which advocates obedience or resignation is too simplistic and rigid.

The ethic of structure complements the ethic of neutrality in attempting to narrow the moral responsibility of individual public servants for the actions of government. This ethic argues that:

> even if administrators may have some scope for independent moral judgement, they cannot be held morally responsible for most of the decisions and policies of government. Their personal moral responsibility extends only to the specific duties of their own office for which they are legally liable.[4]

The premise underlying this ethic is that so many hands are at work, even in the most mundane activity of government, that no one person can be called to account for a particular policy or practice. The complex structure of government, therefore, blunts most efforts to ascribe moral responsibility. It is argued that if you apply an inequitable procedure to an individual applying for social assistance you are not really responsible because you did not contribute to the design and development of the procedure, its acceptance as policy, or the subsequent evaluations of its effectiveness. You are just carrying out your small part of a complicated process.

Thompson's response to this position is to insist on the notion of individual moral responsibility. He points out that it is often possible to pick out the specific acts or omissions of individuals that significantly affected an outcome. Moreover, it is well within our cultural traditions to hold individuals responsible for a deed performed collectively. Under the criminal law, if a group of people assault someone, we don't back away from ascribing individual blame because the crime was a collective act. An official might be excused the first time for following an obviously harmful or unjust procedure; but society would not tolerate repetitions of the procedure. In fact, even if the harmful effects of the procedure were not so obvious, we would have little patience with an official who repeated an action in a rote manner without paying attention to its potential impact.

> **CASE 1.1**
> **IT'S NOT MY PROBLEM**
>
> *Two regional managers in the publicly owned Hydro Corporation are chatting after a staff meeting.*
>
> Bob: I am getting a lot of resistance down the line to this new "get tough" policy with long-term non-performing accounts. These headquarters guys can make it sound like good business, but the bottom line is that we will be cutting off a basic service to people. My folks in the region don't think it's right and, frankly, neither do I.
>
> Fay: Well, it doesn't bother me. If people don't pay or arrange to get some welfare agency to pay for them then they are getting what they deserve. Anyway, it's not our problem. That's what they want in Vancouver, so that's what we do. We don't call the shots. We're cogs in the machine.
>
> Bob: Hmmm. I don't feel that way. My name is on those referral forms. I'm responsible for what goes on in my region. It's too easy just to blame it on Vancouver. I feel like I'm turning off the power myself, sometimes.
>
> Fay: Cool it Bob. Just do your job and relax.
>
> ISSUES
>
> – In a big bureaucracy, is Bob not being a little hard on himself by assuming responsibility for a decision made elsewhere?
> – If you get a legal order from a superior, is there any reason not to follow it?
> – What can Bob do with his conscience in a case like this?

Ethical Relativism: Is There No Right Answer?

If the ethics of neutrality and structure are insufficient to insulate the public servant from personal responsibility for his or her actions, then the need to be able to determine whether conduct is right or wrong becomes self-evident. Public servants must be able to justify their decisions and actions. Before addressing the difficult problem of justification, however, we have to confront two further arguments which muddy the public servant's ethical waters. The first is the notion of relativism; the argument that there are no universally accepted right actions.

The most basic form of ethical relativism occurs where two people agree about the facts of a situation and what is likely to occur if one action is chosen rather than another, but disagree at the level of principle about which action is the right one. This situation arises most starkly if two different cultures are involved (that is, where two individuals come from different societies with distinctly different value structures; as a result they may disagree about the acceptability of practices such as euthanasia, nepotism, or bribery). However, such disagreements can emerge in the context of a single society and even a single organization. Moreover, it is argued by some relativists that such disagreements are not only possible but inevitable because there is no universally accepted approach to ethical reasoning which allows us to deal in a totally convincing way with situations in which the values of one person conflict with the values of another. The ultimate and extreme expression of ethical relativism is the proposition that "if a person *believes* that an action is right for him then he ought to do it" or "if a society or group endorses a certain action in certain circumstances, then that action is right."[5]

The overall thrust of this argument is to undermine the possibility of meaningful disagreements about right and wrong, and the necessity of justifying one's actions. However, a number of counter-arguments have been made to these propositions which tend to cast doubt on some aspects of the relativist position. First, it has been demonstrated that the anthropological evidence supporting ethical relativism is often misleading. It is not as easy as was once thought to demonstrate that individuals from different societies are in conflict on what is the right course of action when faced with a common set of facts. As observation and testing become more sophisticated, accepted practices are reinterpreted and much more uniformity of approach to value problems is observed. Secondly, the notion that an action is right merely because I believe it is right or the group or society of which I am a member endorses it does not stand up to close scrutiny. While my belief that a course of action is right may go some way toward absolving me of blame for any harm I might cause if I pursue that course of action, it is not an adequate basis for determining right. If it were, belief would become an impenetrable substitute for justification, thereby offending our most basic sense about moral judgments: that they must be defensible in forms that other people can understand and debate. The validity of moral judgments implies more than that they are believed to be right by the individual making the judgments.

Hardly more acceptable is the related thesis that an action that a group or a society endorses as right is right for an individual member of that group or society. Again, the major problem with this argument is that it makes disagreements meaningless by setting up the views of the community as the final arbiter of right and wrong. It means that two people can make contradictory judgments ("bribery is right" and "bribery is wrong") and as long as they have the support of two different groups or communities, both statements are compatible. "It follows too that however ignorant or mistaken a given community may be concerning the nature of the action being morally assessed, the statement by a member of a community that the action is right will be true as long as his community does approve of it."[6] Even more damaging to this facet of ethical relativism is the implication that "no member of the society can disagree with his society about the morality of an action . . . Yet it is a fact of moral life that people do sometimes disagree in some instances with what the other members of the society believe regarding moral matters."[7]

Clearly, this relativist position, which attaches such significance to individual or community belief as a basis for value judgments, offends our commonsense approach to moral validity. When we make moral judgments (e.g., "bribery is wrong") we mean more than just "bribery is wrong for me or my community." We mean to say something that has universal validity: "bribery is wrong for everyone."

The third and final point about ethical relativism centres on this issue of universal validity. The relativists force us to confront one important reality: there is, as yet, no form of ethical reasoning which can resolve *all* disputes between conflicting values. This is so even when all the facts and circumstances are agreed upon and both parties to the dispute share a common culture and are impartial, their views untainted by positions derived from class, ethnic, sexual, or ideological considerations. Value conflicts between individuals will remain.

But the impact of this diversity of approaches to ethical reasoning should not be exaggerated. While ethical argument on some issues (e.g., abortion) seem interminable, it is not uncommon for two people arguing from the perspective of two different ethical theories about commonly agreed upon facts and circumstances to see eye to eye on how they should act. Our value conflicts and arguments about the methods to be used to settle them are embedded in a considerable degree of consensus about what is right and what is wrong. This book is an attempt to explore the pluralism of our views about how public servants should act and to point out areas of disagreement and consensus. But the fact of ethical pluralism and society's tolerance for different ethical views should not be seen to lend strength to the advocates of ethical relativism.

Is Public Morality Different from Private Morality?

Before examining the problem of ethical relativism, we noted that there were two arguments that needed airing prior to our exploration of how a public servant might decide whether a proposed action was right or wrong. The second is the argument that administrative ethics or, indeed, any other kind of discrete professional ethics (e.g., business ethics, medical ethics) do not exist and, therefore, do not have to be discussed. According to this argument, no meaningful distinction can or should be made between private morality and public morality. What is right for individuals in their personal dealings with other individuals is right for individuals working within a public or private sector organization.

Those who argue that public and private morality can and should be distinguished usually focus attention on the *role* of the public official. They make a distinction between the general moral rules which apply to individuals as human beings and the duties which arise from roles – such as public servant – which the same individual may fill. Peter Brown argues: "At least some role-related rules impose obligations that conflict with, and sometimes serve as excuses from, obedience to general moral rules."[8] A general prohibition on lying, for instance, might be substantially qualified for a doctor dealing with a terminally ill patient or diplomat involved in negotiations with a hostile power.[9] It was the latter circumstance which inspired the eighteenth-century pun: "An ambassador is an honest man, lying abroad for the good of his country," and, in the nineteenth century, Bismarck's comment: "What a scoundrel a minister would be if, in his own private life, he did half the things he has a duty to do to be true to his oath of office."[10]

The cynicism of such aphorisms should not be allowed to obscure the significance of the public role. While we earlier rejected the notion that the limited role or power of a public servant absolves him or her from individual moral responsibility, in this instance we are arguing that it is this same role which creates a special moral context for the individual public servant. Official roles do not allow public servants to do as they please "for reasons of state" or because "the ends justify the means." However, they do force the public servant to pay attention and give precedence to duties or obligations which are present but often less significant in private morality. In that sense, "dirty hands" may be acceptable where the public good is at stake.

It is because public institutions are designed to further the interests of large numbers of citizens and public acts are divided up among so many public servants that Thomas Nagel argues that public morality is more impersonal than private morality, focusing more attention on attaining the group goals being sought and allowing the public servant greater latitude with respect to the methods used to achieve results. He argues further that "in respect to outcomes, public morality will differ from private in according them more weight." Because of the emphasis placed on success in attaining goals, restrictions on means will be weaker, "permitting the public employment of coercive, manipulative or obstructive methods that would not be allowable for individuals."[11]   Nagel draws particular attention to the special requirement to treat people equally: "Public policies and actions have to be much more impartial than private ones since they usually employ a monopoly of certain kinds of power and since there is no reason in their case to leave room for the personal attachments and inclinations that shape individual lives."[12]

Arguments such as these provide a rationale for the set of duties or principles which this book will explore. The focus on outcomes, for instance, suggests that the public servant needs to consider carefully how he or she defines the public interest when exercising administrative discretion. The emphasis on impartiality will make this value a key consideration in the discussions of political neutrality and service to the public. The possibility that a public servant might justifiably manipulate public opinion in certain circumstances suggests that the duty to hold back confidential information from the public be explored closely. Finally, the potential for coercive behaviour inevitably elevates the duty of accountability to a position of obvious significance.

Not everyone, however, applauds a distinction between public and private morality which, among other things, may countenance an increased tolerance of ruthlessness.[13]   Rejections of the notion of a distinct public morality are usually supported by a host of examples of public officials of unlimited ruthlessness, totally indifferent to widely accepted dictums of personal morality. From the files of European courts, Hitler's Germany, Stalin's Russia, Mackenzie King's wartime government and the modern White House come tales of what happens if office holders are allowed to operate according to moral standards different from those which would apply between two friends. These lurid tales make an important point. Obviously, while wider "means" may be justifiable to reach a desired and legitimate public "end," there are limits. This book is, in fact, about what means are appropriate and

---

CASE 1.2
TO LIE OR NOT TO LIE

The following conversation takes place between two middle mana-gers in a provincial government department.

Cathy: What a mess!

Charlie: It's not as bad as it seems. We can release most of this information. We'll just withhold the three files that could cause trouble.

Cathy: But that would be dishonest!

Charlie: No, it's not. If these files are released they'll be twisted into a scandal by the press. Innocent people will be hurt. The minister and the deputy will be furious. We've got to prevent that. Besides, it's not really lying. We'll just be withholding a piece of information that would distort the truth.

Cathy: It amounts to the same thing.

Charlie: No, it doesn't. Lying is done to cover up something. Our intentions are completely honourable.

Cathy: I still don't like it. I just hate standing up there and lying outright.

Charlie: Trust me. I wouldn't be doing this unless I really believed it was for the good of all concerned. This isn't girl guides any more, Cathy. Sometimes you just have to lie.

ISSUES

– Should Cathy be more "flexible" in this case?

– Under what conditions is it appropriate for a public servant to lie?

– Are the ethical rules you follow in your private life generally good guides to the way you should act as a public servant? If not, why not?

what ends are desirable. The advocates of a distinct public morality don't advocate or condone undue ruthlessness. All they argue is that the *balance* of what is acceptable may be different in the public sector than in private life. The tools of ethical reasoning used to make such determinations in public decision-making are the same as those used in matters of private morality, but certain considerations will be of more weight in the former than the latter.

Justifying Value Choices

In our earlier discussions, two rather simple avenues to problem-solving which public servants regularly rely upon have been found wanting. First, the notion that public servants can legitimately solve all tough value choices by blindly following the relevant law or their supervisor's interpretation of policies or traditional principles of behaviour is unacceptable. Obviously, some public servants will rarely confront a problem in which following the law or guidelines for behaviour laid down by their government or superiors is not the responsible thing to do. But as a matter of principle, laws, orders, or endorsement by superiors do not provide an individual public servant with an adequate justification for an action that he or she suspects is ethically questionable. What is legal is not always right, and commonly accepted rules of behaviour can easily be "interpreted" to support questionable actions.

Secondly, a lot of people take a rather rough and tumble approach to deciding whether a particular action is right or wrong. Their simple operating rule is: "Don't do anything you wouldn't want to read about in your local newspaper in the morning." This maxim is a variation on advice which Harry Truman gave to a Senate committee witness during the Second World War: "Generals should never do anything that needs to be explained to a Senate committee."[14] The "ethics of prudence," as Peter Drucker refers to it, directs public officials to "shun actions that cannot easily be understood, explained or justified."

While this approach to ethical decision-making may have a certain populist charm, its democratic base is also its undoing. As Drucker points out:

> Concern with what one can justify becomes, only too easily, concern with appearances – Machiavelli was by no means the first to point out that in a "Prince," that is, in someone in

authority and high visibility, appearances may matter more than substance. The Ethics of Prudence thus easily decay into the hypocrisy of "public relations."[15]

Unfortunately, because the mass of the public may react negatively to the media's portrayal of your decision does not make it the wrong ethical decision – in anything other than the political sense. The obverse is equally true. Right and wrong cannot necessarily be determined or justified by votes.

Constitutions, Economic Theory, and the Rule of Law as Arbiters of Right and Wrong

"Since the focus of our inquiry is the ethics of one very specific role, it seems that the moral foundation we are looking for must be tailored to the demands of that limited role."[16]   From this unexceptionable premise, John Rohr goes on to argue that public servants should base their justification of good and bad behaviour on the values of the regime within which they work. In the Canadian context, they should search for the driving values of the federation in a systematic way in such places as the constitution (including the Charter of Rights and Freedoms and provincial constitutional legislation), Supreme Court decisions, the speeches of statesmen, and so on. Where mutually exclusive values seem relevant to a particular dilemma confronted by the public servant, Rohr argues that "he will have to choose the position he finds most appealing and persuasive . . . Just how those values are interpreted is a decision only the bureaucrat himself can make."[17]

There's the rub! We have seen this argument before in our discussion of relativism and the ethic of neutrality. We raise it again in this context because it helps to emphasize a number of important points about justification. First, the traditional principles of the "seven commandments" which we will be examining in subsequent chapters are all based on normative theories. "Be politically neutral" and "be accountable" are principles derived from the theory of responsible cabinet government. Similarly, the admonition to provide the public with fair and impartial service is rooted in the rule of law and the theory of natural justice; and the insistence on efficiency traces its roots to microeconomic and scientific management theories. Unfortunately, none of these theories on their own provides clear enough directions about how principles are to be interpreted in specific situations. Moreover, none provides much help when a value (e.g., fairness) from one theory (e.g., natural justice) collides with a value (e.g., efficiency) from another (e.g., microeconomics). In a limited way constitutional, economic, and legal theory can provide guidance in ethical dilemmas, but more fundamental means of thinking about value conflicts are required. Terry Cooper approvingly quotes Row and Egger on this key point: "An administrator needs 'some bench marks for relating the various and frequently conflicting claims of competing values which enter into his official actions.' These will not be provided by the law, the courts or delegated authority: they are too general in nature."[18]

Focusing on Consequences and Duty

If we ignore the followers of emotivism (who argue that ethical judgments are nothing more than statements of personal preference) and the followers of existentialism (who view the world as irrational and life as ultimately meaningless), most ethical philosophers have approached the justification of ethical positions as teleologists or deontologists. The former, also referred to as naturalists, defend an action or rule as right by relating it to observable phenomena such as the hedonistic satisfaction of desire (Hobbes and Spinoza), the production of pleasure for the greatest number (Bentham and Mill), or the fostering of historical progress (Marx). The teleological approach grounds ethical action in human nature and the fulfilment of biological and social needs: an action or rule is right because of its propensity to produce desired results. Deontologists, the non-naturalists, are reluctant to ground ethical decisions in observable phenomena. Instead, they look outside nature for support for ethical assertions, finding it in *a priori* laws and reason (Kant), divine law (St. Augustine and St. Thomas Aquinas), and intuition (Sidgwick and Ross).[19] For deontologists, the nature of the act itself (e.g., lying) is far more relevant to its justification or condemnation than the consequences which flow from it.

One of the most widely employed teleological approaches to ethical justification focuses on consequences or outcomes. Utilitarianism is the most common form of consequentialist ethical theory. The basic thesis driving utilitarianism is well understood: what is right is the principle, rule, or action which produces – or tends to produce – the greatest amount of good for the greatest number of people. The essence of moral calculus according to utilitarianism is to determine which course of action has the maximum net benefits (or the minimum net costs) for the relevant stakeholders – that is, *everyone* who is significantly affected by it. Equality is a key component of the utilitarian calculus. The focus is on maximizing the good of all. No particular person's or group's "good" is any more important than the good of any other person or group. As Jeremy Bentham put it, "everybody to count for one, nobody for more than one."

Some proponents of this approach want to focus the calculus on individual actions or decisions (act utilitarians), while others (rule utilitarians) are content to endorse rules or principles that have tended consistently in the past to produce the most good. The latter approach removes the need to apply a detailed analysis to each action contemplated. Regardless of the variation adopted, the common thread is the identification of the right action – one's duty – with that alternative which maximizes the good.

The problems with the utilitarian approach are also well known. Anyone familiar with the complexities of cost-benefit analysis applied to even an apparently simple problem will appreciate the mechanical difficulties confronting such calculations in the context of a complicated value dilemma. Identifying everyone who is likely to be significantly affected either directly or indirectly by a decision, weighting their various concerns, establishing all the likely consequences of the various possible actions, and calculating net benefits and costs in the context of concerns expressed are not likely to be simple tasks in most instances.

But mechanical difficulties associated with implementation are not enough to sink an ethical theory. It is also argued that utilitarianism does not clarify whether very positive outcomes for a small number should outweigh an inconvenience for many. Put another way, utilitarianism, in its fixation with maximizing good, seems overly preoccupied with efficiency and indifferent to distributional considerations involving merit and need. This concern is related to the charge that utilitarianism seems to favour the adoption of actions which violate our basic sense of justice. The classic example is the sheriff who chooses to turn a suspected criminal over to a lynch mob because to do otherwise would precipitate a riot and lead to the loss of several lives. This consequentially based decision, it is argued, flies in the face of the widely accepted notion that it is the sheriff's duty to protect prisoners in his custody. It raises the wider criticism that utilitarianism focuses too much on the consequences or ends (it is called "end-point ethics" by some), and ignores the means by which these ends are achieved.

Utilitarians counter arguments such as these by pointing out that simple examples often misrepresent the utilitarian calculus. A utilitarian would argue that if the goal of maintaining and increasing respect for the law was considered by the sheriff, he might decide to hold on to the prisoner. However, that same utilitarian would insist that you can justify the violation of a widely respected practice (e.g., the protection of prisoners) if the benefits of doing so clearly outweigh the costs of adhering to that practice. Similarly, it would be noted that a sophisticated utilitarian is not blind to distributional considerations. Given the diminishing marginal utility of any good, the utilitarian calculus is bound to favour the distribution of goods to the least advantaged. Because of the significance attached to self-esteem by utilitarians, there is a strong presumption in favour of equal treatment.

The major alternative to an outcomes approach to the justification of an action or rule is one which focuses on the nature of the action or the rule itself. Two important features of the deontological (or "duty") approach are its reliance on overriding moral principles which are dictated by reason, and its preoccupation with the rights of individuals. Actions and rules are right because they are intrinsically or inherently right, not because of the social good they produce. For deontologists, the basic needs and rights of individuals as individuals are more important than the maximization of overall good.

Not all deontologists approach the justification of moral duty the same way. Natural law theorists see basic moral precepts as reflecting the inclinations which have been instilled in each human being by God or nature. We discover the obligations to be honest, tell the truth, preserve human life, act justly and keep promises through reason, revelation, or empirical observation; we follow such precepts regardless of their consequences because they represent a divine or natural standard of right human behaviour.

Another variation on this theme is intuitionism. W.D. Ross and others argue that a number of key ethical principles are self-evident; that is to say, they are plainly true to a rational, mature person.[20] These include utilitarian principles such as promoting the happiness of oneself and others and refraining from harm to other people, as well as more traditional standards such as telling the truth, keeping promises, and showing gratitude. While intuitionists do not always agree on which principles are self-evident, they do come together around the notion that such principles represent *prima facie* duties; in other words, they are duties that must be carried out unless more compelling moral obligations intervene. They argue that this approach is more defensible than utilitarianism because it recognizes the fact that principles other than those relating to consequences are important to people when they confront moral choices.

Immanuel Kant developed the most widely known version of the argument that right and wrong can (and must) be determined without reference to the consequences of particular actions. According to Kant, moral law is to be found in human reason. To be moral is to act rationally. Since reason is common to all human beings, moral duty would be the same for each individual, and each individual has within himself or herself the capacity to discover morality. Therefore ethics articulates rationally based moral laws which all rational individuals would be bound to follow.

But how do we discover whether a specific moral rule or action is right? Kant's rational tool or test for determining morality is the categorical imperative. An action or rule is right (or becomes a duty) if it meets the criteria set down by the the categorical imperative. These criteria are reflected in three complementary but distinct formulations of the categorical imperative.

- An action or rule is right if it can be made universal. Alternately, an action or rule would be morally wrong if you could not accept the notion of everyone following it. Kant did not want a person to act in ways that would make him or her the exception. A public servant contemplating whistle-blowing as a response to a particular situation should consider whether it would be acceptable for everyone to blow the whistle on superiors in similar circumstances.

- An action or rule is right if it treats individuals as ends in themselves. This formulation of the categorical imperative focuses our attention on the idea that all persons are rational beings and cannot, therefore, be used by us – in our private or official capacities – as means to an end. The emphasis here is on equality and the irrationality of our being allowed to act in ways which deprive others of their rights. These rights include, for many commentators, not only the basic rights to life, freedom, and property, but the wider spectrum of political, legal, economic, and social rights fostered by a contemporary liberal democracy. We are constantly being confronted with cases in which the positive and widespread societal consequences of actions are juxtaposed against their corrosive effects on "the integrity of the person as a freely choosing entity."[21] Kant and others want to draw our attention to the significance of the rights of the individual.

- A final variation on this theme is that an action or rule is right if you would be prepared to have the action or rule directed at yourself. Put another way, you should act as if you were a member of a community and might wake up the next morning as the subject of the action. If you are contemplating a reduction in the welfare payments to certain citizens, would you still be prepared to approve that action if you were the welfare recipient and subject to the new regulations? This statement of the theme places a high priority on the notions of fairness and reciprocity and, to borrow a now famous phrase from John Rawls, insists that we make decisions about public policy and administrative practice from behind a "veil of ignorance" concerning our own place in society.[22]

The parallels between the categorical imperative – or ultimate moral principle – and the golden rule (do unto others as they should do unto you), the Confucian rule of reciprocity, and Rabbi Hillel's saying (what is hateful to you do not do to your neighbour) are obvious and significant. In a sense, contemporary deontological ethics are a reason and individual centred restatement (or "ghost")[23] of the traditional Judeo-Christian morality founded on the divinely revealed commandments.

What are the major problems with the deontological approach to establishing the rightness or wrongness of rules or actions such as the ones we will be looking at in subsequent chapters? The first problem is one that afflicts utilitarianism as well. If a fundamental rule (e.g., maximize happiness, treat people as ends) is not indubitably proved, then why should it be viewed as the ultimate arbiter of right and wrong? The fact that deontologists do not agree on a list of fundamental rules suggests that reason may not be an adequate guide to ultimate moral criteria.

More crucial from our more limited perspective is the capacity of the Kantian principle or the intuitionist's fundamental moral rules to deal with clashes of duties or rights. Utilitarianism has trouble choosing between actions or rules which do a lot of good for a few or a little good for many. Similarly, deontological ethics provides little assistance when you are faced with the situation where fundamental rules are in conflict or the rights of two different groups or individuals cannot *both* be met by any of the actions or rules which might apply. For instance, increasing the right of some citizens to have access to information held by government may decrease the right to privacy of other citizens, groups and corporations. Both rights may be legitimate according to the deontological litmus test, but the test doesn't help us much with the issue of settling conflicts between them.

Looking Ahead to Problem-Solving

While neither of these two approaches to justification is entirely satisfactory, they are also not entirely at war with each other. In many cases, as we noted earlier, applying both approaches would bring you to the same conclusion. The key feature of both the utilitarian and deontological frameworks is that they force public servants to rise above laziness, bias, and the routine of following orders or laws without thought when faced with difficult value dilemmas. In many circumstances traditional rules will provide adequate guidance to what is right. But in many other circumstances, individuals will have to be alert to the consequences and inherent morality of their actions. This thumbnail sketch of two fundamental ethical theories does not presume to provide public servants with the equipment they need to become sophisticated ethical analysts, but it should make them sensitive to what is at stake when confronted with a value dilemma.

The most basic duty of a public servant is to pay attention to such dilemmas. Once the dilemma is recognized, what steps should the responsible public servant take? An orderly approach to reaching a "reflective equilibrium" would include the following:[24]

- Clarifying the facts of the situation. Many value dilemmas disappear when the facts are made clear.

- Coming up with a considered view on how to act. Such a view is intuitive and may exhibit "moral imagination," but it is not simple emotion.

- Establishing the rule or rules which seem to apply to the situation. This will lead inevitably to an effort to bring the individual's considered view and the rules together. This process has been referred to as establishing "narrow reflective equilibrium" because it is essentially conservative, working within the confines of existing rules and practices, and does not question the appropriateness of these rules or practices.

- However, if a fit between a considered view about how to act and the rules which seem to apply to the particular situation proves difficult to create, or more than one rule seems to apply to the situation, the individual is forced to move to the level of fundamental theory and seek guidance by asking some basic utilitarian or deontological questions (or both) about the alternative courses of action suggested and the relevant rules.

A brief example of an attempt to establish reflective equilibrium may help to bring this important process to life. Suppose a public servant is faced with a situation in which his superiors in the transportation regulatory agency for which he is an air safety analyst refuse his request to release information related to the safety of air travel. The facts seem clear enough: citizens are making potentially dangerous travel plans because they do not have the access to relevant information which has been declared confidential. The intuitive reaction might be to conclude that a way must be found to provide that information to the travelling public. However, the operative rule within the organization is to keep confidential information confidential. Moreover, this rule is endorsed by a number of professional codes of conduct, including the Statement of Principles Regarding the Conduct of Public Employees issued by the Institute of Public Administration of Canada (see Appendix). The Statement of Principles also stresses the public servant's duty of loyalty to the government. The public servant reviews the facts, his considered view, and the applicable professional "commandments," but can find no way to bring them into harmony. He believes that his intuitive reaction is well grounded in a general moral obligation not to expose people to risk without their consent. Even the Statement of Principles recognizes that in some instances the public servant must depend on what his individual conscience tells him is right.

At this point he turns to his ethical tool kit for assistance. Looking at the problem from a consequentialist perspective, he sees that the risk to travellers is real but statistically small. On the other hand, the release of the information might have a devastating impact on the credibility and effectiveness of the agency and the profitability and viability of the air transport industry. From a deontological perspective, however, he is impressed by the compelling power of the *prima facie* duty not to expose people to risk without their consent. Moreover, he recognizes that he would see it as a fundamental violation of his rights to be placed in the situation of the average citizen making travel plans without access to the information in question. Which way should he go to achieve "reflective equilibrium"? What should he do if he concludes that the information must be made available to the public but his superiors do not agree?

As this example suggests, the interplay of considered views, rules, and theories is often difficult to follow and rarely leads to unequivocal answers. It is unusual that one value or duty obviously "trumps" another. This is especially true in the group or committee context in which so many government decisions are made. On the other side, however, to ignore the obligation to confront difficult ethical dilemmas and unclear or inappropriate rules is to ignore the essence of responsible public service.

Notes

1. David Zussman, *Confidence in Canadian Government Institutions* (Halifax: IRPP, 1988).

2. See Peter Aucoin, "Administrative Reform in Public Management: Paradigms, Principles, Paradoxes and Pendulums," a paper prepared for the IPSA Conference on Contemporary Governmental Structures, Universidad Autonoma de Madrid, Madrid, May 1989.

3. Dennis F. Thompson, "The Possibility of Administrative Ethics," *Public Administration Review* 45 (September/October 1985), p. 556.

4. Ibid, p. 559.

5. See B. Brandt, "Ethical Relativism" in Paul Edwards, ed., *The Encyclopedia of Philosophy* 3 (New York: Macmillan, 1967), pp. 75-78. Much of the argument on relativism is drawn from Brandt's entry.

6. Jonathan Harrison, "Ethical Subjectivism" in ibid., p. 78.

7. Richard T. de George, *Business Ethics*, 2nd ed. (New York: Macmillan, 1986).

8. Peter Brown, "Assessing Officials" in J.L. Fleishman et al., eds., *Public Duties: the Moral Obligations of Government Officials* (Cambridge: Harvard University Press, 1981), p. 290.

9. Sisela Bok deals with both examples in her important book on lying. S. Bok, *Lying* (New York: Vintage Books, 1979).

10. Cited in Peter F. Drucker, "What Is 'Business Ethics,'" *Across the Board* (October 1981), p. 27. Neither, in this context, would one want to ignore a remark attributed to John Maynard Keynes: "An official is a man who has his ear so close to the ground that he cannot hear what an upright man says."

11. Thomas Nagel, "Ruthlessness in Public Life" in S. Hampshire, ed., *Public and Private Morality* (Cambridge: Cambridge University Press, 1978), p. 84.

12. Ibid.

13. For a powerful argument against the acceptability of "dirty hands" see Dennis F. Thompson, *Political Ethics and Public Office* (Cambridge: Harvard University Press, 1987), ch. 1.

14. Quoted in Drucker, "What Is 'Business Ethics,'" p. 28.

15. Ibid.

16. John A. Rohr, "The Study of Ethics in the P.A. Curriculum," *Public Administration Review* 36 (July/August 1976), p. 400.

17. Ibid., pp. 404-5.

18. Terry L. Cooper, *The Responsible Administrator* (Port Washington, N.Y.: Kennikat Press, 1982), p. 54.

19. This overview is drawn largely from R. Abelson and K. Nielsen, "The History of Ethics" in Edwards, *Encyclopedia of Philosophy*, vols. 3 and 4, pp. 81-116.

20. See W.D. Ross, *The Right and the Good* (Oxford: Oxford University Press, 1930).

21. Charles Fried, *Right and Wrong* (Cambridge, Mass.: Harvard University Press, 1978), p. 109.

22. John Rawls, *A Theory of Justice* (Cambridge, Mass.: Harvard University Press, 1971).

23. See Alasdair MacIntyre, *After Virtue* (Notre Dame: University of Notre Dame Press, 1981), p. 105.

24. This process is outlined in Brown, "Assessing Officials," p. 294.

Chapter 2

Acting in the Public Interest

Public servants are frequently advised to "act in the public interest." Yet there is a vigorous and enduring debate over what the public interest means and whether it serves any useful purpose as a guide to appropriate conduct in the public sector. It is important, therefore, to explain as precisely as possible what is meant by the concept of the public interest. In the context of our focus on the responsible public servant, is the concept a useful one? Does "act in the public interest" mean anything more than "act responsibly"? Is the determination of the public interest really any of the public servant's business? If it is, can the notion of the public interest provide practical guidance for bureaucratic decision-making? Each of these questions will be considered in this chapter.

The Public Interest in the Real World

Public servants receive conflicting messages regarding their duty to act in the public interest. Frequently, they are advised or required to establish what the public interest is and to safeguard it. On other occasions, however, they are told to adhere to the ethic of neutrality,

33

that is, to remember that determining the public interest is the job of elected politicians, not of public servants.

The message that public servants should seek out and protect the public interest is often set down in government statutes, regulations, guidelines, and other documents. For example, the federal Combines Investigation Act gives public servants the responsibility of identifying and taking action against illegal mergers (those involving "acquisition or control of a business . . . whereby competition . . . is likely to be lessened to the detriment or against the interest of the public, whether consumers, producers or others"). The Ontario Statutory Procedures Act allows closed hearings when the tribunal decides that "the desirability of avoiding disclosure of certain information . . . in the public interest outweighs the desirability of adhering to the principle that hearings be open to the public." And the federal Public Service Commission notes that "the notion of the public interest calls for Public Service employment policies, processes and practices based on five basic principles": efficiency and effectiveness, sensitivity and responsiveness, equality of access, equity, and merit.[1] Such instructions leave lots of room for interpretation as to what the public interest means and for the balancing of competing values.

Some codes of ethics for public servants draw attention to the public servant's obligation to act in the public interest. For example, the *Conflict of Interest Policy for Manitoba Government Employees* notes that "by providing clear standards of employee conduct, the guidelines aim at safeguarding the public interest." And the *Employee Code of Ethics for the City of Edmonton* states that "employees must observe the highest ethical standards in the performance of their duties. The public interest must be their primary concern." Similarly, the Statement of Principles of the Institute of Public Administration of Canada (see Appendix) advises public servants that they "should resolve any conflict between their personal or private interests and their official duties in favour of the public interest."

A conflicting message to public servants is that while serving the public interest is a primary duty, its determination may not be their concern; rather it is the concern of the elected officials to whom they report. According to the ethic of neutrality[2] explained in chapter 1, public servants do not have to exercise independent judgment as to the content of the public interest because they are expected to perform their duties in a neutral, objective, and impartial manner. They are to be neutral not only in the sense of being non-partisan but also in the sense of not making value judgments as to which policy options are preferable, that is, "in the public interest." It is argued that public servants should simply implement policies decided upon by elected officials; where public servants have authority to make decisions on their own, they do so within a framework of values provided by these officials. This position is also reflected in the Institute's Statement of Principles when it states that "public employees should seek to serve the public interest by upholding both the letter and the spirit of the laws established by the legislature or council and of the regulations and directions made pursuant to these laws."

For Canada's public servants this ethic of neutrality is defined at the federal and provincial levels by the rules of the Westminster model on which the Canadian system of government is based. If the Canadian system of government operated as some idealized versions of the Westminster model suggest it should, the public interest, as expressed through policy decisions and laws, would be determined by elected officials, notably cabinet ministers. Establishing the content of the public interest would *not* be the business of the public servant. In reality, however, the Canadian system does not operate in strict accordance with the Westminster model. (Indeed, neither does the British system.) It is now widely recognized in Canadian society that public servants exercise very significant power in the political system, both in developing public policies and implementing them. As a result, public servants, especially at the middle to upper levels of the administrative hierarchy, have many opportunities to make recommendations and decisions as to how the public interest can best be served. An important source of bureaucratic power is expertise based on education, experience, and access to information. Both political executives and legislators are obliged to rely on public servants for advice and decisions on policies and programs. Another important source of bureaucratic power is the legitimacy of the public servants' advisory and decision-making roles; ministers, of course, have the authority to reject bureaucratic advice and to alter bureaucratic decisions.

Public servants exercise their considerable discretionary powers in several ways. They influence the content of legislation by initiating policy proposals and by preparing policy options at the request of political or administrative superiors; they pass regulations under authority delegated to them by ministers and legislators and they interpret, apply, clarify, amend, and enforce these regulations; they consult and negotiate with individuals and groups seeking to influence government decisions and expenditures; they mobilize support for their policies and programs; and on occasion they resist changes and innovations desired by their political superiors. The significant power wielded by public servants means that the values they bring to the decision-making process and the criteria they use to resolve value conflicts are critically important to the determination of the public interest. Certainly, public servants make a great number of routine decisions which have little apparent value content, but they also make many decisions where the value implications are as important as technical, financial, managerial, or political considerations. Thus, both the determination and the protection of the public interest are necessarily very much the public servants' business.

The Utility of the Public Interest

The acceptance of the public servant's real-world involvement in determining and protecting the public interest does not immediately clear the way for us to make operational the duty to act in the public interest. The reason is that for a number of commentators the degree to which public servants are exhorted to seek out and protect the public interest does little to mitigate a more fundamental problem: the elusiveness of the concept. J.E. Hodgetts notes that the public interest is not only "slippery, mercurial and possessed of the qualities of the chameleon; it is akin to the Holy Grail, in that its relevance for political life may reside in the pursuit and anticipation rather than in the actual grasping or attainment of the reality it is supposed to represent."[3] Thus, the efforts of public servants to serve the public interest may often appear to be a quest for an ethereal goal.

Some theorists contend that the concept is so elusive as to be meaningless and irrelevant. Glendon Schubert, after a systematic review of interpretations and explanations of the public interest, concluded that there was no "statement of public-interest theory that offers much promise either as a guide to public officials who are supposed to make decisions in the public interest, or to research scholars who might wish to investigate the extent to which governmental decisions are empirically made in the public interest."[4] Schubert is only one of a number of theorists who have concluded that the notion of the public interest is not a credible one. This school of thought has been described as the "abolitionists."[5]   A leading representative of this school, Arthur F. Bentley, has referred to the public interest and the general welfare as "mindstuff, appropriately discussed by writers of fiction who spun fantasies, but with no place in the reality which it was the business of the social scientist to explore."[6]

The abolitionists emphasize the central importance of interest groups in politics. In their view, government decisions result from competition among the interests of individuals and groups seeking to maximize their self-interest. They claim that there is no such thing as the public interest or the common good; rather there are only the various interests of many publics. Moreover, they interpret interests as preferences or wants; thus, selfish interests cannot be distinguished from altruistic interests.

The public choice theorists have joined in the assault on the concept of the public interest. A central element of public choice theory is that all political actors, including public servants, act in a rational, self-interested manner. Thus, it is argued, bureaucratic behaviour can best be explained in terms of public servants seeking such selfish objectives as power, income, and prestige. Such concepts as the public interest and the general will are viewed as "mystical notions."[7] Even altruism is explained in terms of a self-interested search for personal satisfaction.

Despite these criticisms of the concept of the public interest, a large number of political theorists, whom we may call the "preservationists," view it as a viable and, indeed, a valuable concept. They believe that the concept has important effects on the operation of political systems and the content of public policies. The public interest has been defined as a "spur to conscience and to deliberation"[8] and as what people "would choose if they saw clearly, thought rationally, acted disinterestedly and benevolently."[9] It should be viewed as an ethical standard by which public policies are evaluated. C.W. Cassinelli, for example, describes the public interest as "the highest ethical standard applicable to political affairs."[10] Most preservationists view people "as social beings who form associations, including political associations, for a better common life and not simply for private benefits." They do not just form interest groups seeking private interest; rather they form communities seeking a common good (the public interest). As a result, "the normative standard by which a proposed public policy must be evaluated is whether it will contribute more to the common good than alternative policies."[11]

In practice, the concept of the public interest is widely used; it has strong emotional appeal and far-reaching consequences. Certainly, individuals and organizations wishing to influence government decisions are encouraged or obliged to couch their arguments in terms of the broad public interest as opposed to narrow, selfish or personal interests. We turn now to an examination of the extent to which the concept of the public interest can serve as a practical guide to responsible administrative behaviour.

The Public Interest as an Operational Guide

The following argument proceeds on the assumption that the preservationists are correct in their contention that the public interest is a credible concept, one worth retaining. "Act in the public interest" may at root mean no more than "act responsibly," but the concept of the public interest has become the centre of an important commandment in its own right. It has also bred its own distinctive set of approaches by which the concept can be brought to life and used to figure out where the public good lies among a host of competing policy options.

This section examines four approaches to decision-making in the public interest. These are the *dominant value, procedural, consensualist,* and *cost-benefit* approaches. To assess the usefulness of these various interpretations, readers are encouraged to consider the three cases contained in this chapter in light of the guidance provided by each approach. In these approaches to the public interest and in the language they employ, readers will easily identify variations on the basic deontological and utilitarian approaches to ethical problem solving which were explored in chapter 1. In particular, the dominant value, procedural, and consensualist approaches have much in common with deontological theory, whereas the cost-benefit approach is in essence an application of utilitarian theory.

The Dominant Value Approach

The dominant value approach attempts to provide guidance for determining the substantive content of the public interest in particular circumstances. A particular value (e.g., justice, freedom, equality, human dignity) is used as the ultimate criterion, or at least as a critically important criterion, for deciding what actions are in the public interest.

For example, the criterion of *justice-as-fairness* has been presented as the overriding value by which the public interest should be determined. Justice-as-fairness is the central concept in the work of the philosopher John Rawls. He argues that two principles of justice should be applied to determine the public interest. The first principle is that "each person is to have an equal right to the most extensive total system of equal basic liberties compatible with a similar system of liberty for all." The second principle is that "social and economic inequalities are to be arranged so that they are both: a) to the greatest benefit of the least advantaged ... and b) attached to offices and positions open to all under conditions of fair equality of opportunity."[12] In the event that these principles clash with one another, the first principle is to have precedence. Rawls argues that "social and economic inequalities, for example, inequalities of wealth and authority, are just only if they result in compensating benefits for everyone, and in particular for the least advantaged members of society." Moreover, "these principles rule out justifying institutions on the grounds that the hardships of some are offset by a greater good in the aggregate. It may be expedient but it is not just that some should have less in order that others may prosper."[13] Note the striking contrast between Rawls's position and utilitarian ethical theory.

The concrete application of Rawls's theory can be demonstrated by reference to case 2.1 which involves the hiring, training, and advancement of a member of a group which is disadvantaged in society and underrepresented in the public service. Rawls would present the following argument. Hiring and promoting Cary achieves basic liberty for her but does not infringe on the basic liberty of others. If Cary were not hired, one of society's most disadvantaged persons would be further disadvantaged. By hiring Cary, the government demonstrates its commitment to having its "positions and offices open to all." Finally, by hiring Cary, who is one of "the least advantaged members of society," the government is trying to ensure that its positions and offices are allocated in a way which is "reasonably ... to everyone's advantage."

Is it reasonable to expect public servants to apply Rawls's two principles of justice to their decision-making? Or is a more practical

---

CASE 2.1
PUBLIC INTEREST OR SELF INTEREST?

In this case, Sean and Leslie chat about a colleague's recent promotion.

Sean: I just have to blow off steam – but I wouldn't want this to get around.

Leslie: Go ahead. I'm all ears.

Sean: Well, you know Cary. First, she gets a permanent job with the public service – no temporary position, no competition, no hassle. Then, she gets weeks and weeks of middle management training. Courses I'd love to attend, if I had the time and could get permission. So I'm minding memos, doing my job, paying my dues, while she's taking courses. Next I find out that she's being fast-tracked and will probably be a director within two years!

Why? All because she's native and we've got the Indigenous Development Program. I know it's right and we need affirmative action and role models for our native people but... The bottom line is that I'm jealous. I'm more qualified and more experienced but I won't get offered the chance to compete for a director's position for a long time. There's less opportunity for advancement than there used to be. Frankly, I'm thinking of talking to the boss about it.

Leslie: Okay, I sympathize. But the other side of this is that native people have been shut out of the system. They need special programs so that managers will consider them. There's probably more racism out there than we realize. Besides, you may be better qualified than she is, but she is fully qualified for the job for which she was hired.

Besides, she might not be successful. She's trying to adjust to a new job, the course work is demanding, and she's afraid that other people in the office resent the assistance she's getting. Sometimes I wonder if she's being set up to fail. She's under a lot of pressure.

Sean: I wouldn't want that to happen to anybody. And I can see that her perspective on policy issues is needed. Plus her experience and contacts in the native political community are valuable, no question about it. But I still believe that I deserve a chance before she does.

ISSUES

– Is Sean simply allowing his self-interest to blind him to the wider public interest?

. . . /cont'd

```
┌─────────────────────────────────────────────────────────┐
│                    CASE 2.1 (cont'd)                    │
├─────────────────────────────────────────────────────────┤
```

- Should individuals or groups be compensated for past discrimination or deprivation?
- Is it fair to deny a member of a majority group what he or she would have normally received if affirmative action was not operating?
- What do you do when faced with developing policy or delivering programs in the face of such incompatible values?

guide to the public interest to be found in Rawls's notion of "the veil of ignorance": the notion that we should make decisions as if we didn't know what our lot in life is or will be? For example, in the sphere of employment equity, the decision-maker would adopt the perspective of someone who didn't know whether he or she was an advantaged or disadvantaged person. Would this approach make decision makers more sensitive to the concerns of disadvantaged persons?

Members of the New Public Administration movement which emerged in the United States in the early 1970s look with approval upon Rawls's theory because it supports their emphasis on the desirability of emphasizing *social equity* in public administration. Social equity "includes activities designed to enhance the political power and economic well-being of (disadvantaged) minorities." It is generally viewed as a contending value rather than as the overriding value by which the public interest should be determined. Thus it should be pursued along with such traditional public administration values as economy, efficiency and responsiveness. *"New Public Administration seeks not only to carry out legislative mandates as efficiently and effectively as possible, but to both influence and execute policies which more generally improve the quality of life for all."*[14] Public servants are encouraged to ask themselves whether the service they are providing to the public enhances social equity.

Dvorin and Simmons, who fall within the broad category of New Public Administration scholars, argue that the concept of *human dignity* should be the ultimate criterion of the public interest. Radical humanism is offered as the frame of reference within which this concept of the public interest may emerge. Radical humanism requires "the ultimate capitulation of operational mechanics and political strategies to a concept of the public interest based on man as *the* most important concern of bureaucratic power."[15] Does exhorting public servants to enhance human dignity provide them with better guidance than urging them to pursue the public interest?

Among the values often singled out as the ultimate criterion for determining the public interest are values such as liberty and equality, which are closely tied to particular political ideologies. We know that the ideological commitments of public servants influence their recommendations and decisions on public policy[16] and we know that these commitments have a significant effect on policy decisions in such areas as the redistribution of income, employment programs, and human rights. Do we want public servants emphasizing values such as liberty or equality as the overriding value in their decision-making calculus? Is it appropriate for them to inject an ideological preference into the policy process? What if this preference is not shared by their political superiors? Is it important that ideological preferences be made explicit in bureaucratic decision-making so that they can be openly weighed against other values? Is the public interest to be found in the reconciliation of competing values rather than in the application of a single dominant value?

The Procedural Approach

The procedural approach suggests that the public interest is found in the reconciliation of the conflicting interests surrounding a particular issue if certain standards of procedure are followed in the decision-making process. If these standards (e.g., the democratic process, administrative due process) are followed, the rights of those affected are protected by the process. Schubert explains that "people accept democratic decision-making processes because these provide the maximum opportunity for diverse interests to seek to influence governmental decisions at all levels ... *Decisions that are the product of a process of full consideration are most likely to be decisions in the public interest.*"[17]

Advocates of this approach argue that there should be procedures in the political process to make sure that all groups affected by a public policy have access to government decision-makers and that this access is granted as equitably as possible. Public servants are encouraged to ask such questions as these: Is the decision-making process fair to all interests? Have I provided adequate access for individuals and groups wishing to be heard? Have I provided all possible relevant information?

The Consensualist Approach

The consensualist approach is an extension of the procedural approach. It reminds public servants that the public interest is broader than the sum of the interests of those who are well represented in the decision-making process. Account must be taken of the interests of individuals and groups who are unrepresented or underrepresented in the policy process. The public interest is made up of more than private interests and self-interest; it must even take account of the interests of future generations.[18] Anthony Downs asserts that the public interest is "closely related to the minimal consensus necessary for the operation of a democratic society. This consists of an implicit agreement among the preponderance of the people concerning two main areas: the basic rules of conduct and decision-making that should be followed in the society; and general principles regarding the fundamental social policies that the government ought to carry out."[19] J.E. Hodgetts makes a similar argument in his assertion that mankind's pursuit of the public interest "has been a search for consensus – the hard core of accepted values and traditions that holds a community together, enabling it to pursue common objectives."[20]

The consensualist approach prompts public servants who are seeking the public interest to ask themselves: Have I taken account of all affected interests and not just those of well-represented groups? Have I kept in mind the good of the community as well the interests of groups and individuals? Have I considered carefully enough the possible long-range effects of my decision?

The Cost-Benefit Approach

This approach views the public interest as emerging from cost-benefit analysis. This is a technique used to evaluate policy options by determining for each option the ratio of benefits to costs or the difference between benefits and costs. The option which best serves the public interest is the one whose benefits exceed its costs by the

CASE 2.2
THE RISK OF EXPOSURE

The following conversation takes place between Morena, an engineer employed by Expo, and Alan, an Expo vice-president for operations.

Morena: A week ago, I got a call from a guy claiming that he knew for a fact that the asphalt used to pave the Expo site is contaminated with PCBs. He said that a lot of the gravel used in the asphalt had come from an area where there was a large PCB spill not long ago.

Alan: I didn't hear about that.

Morena: Neither did I. But he told me that the spill had been hushed up. The whole idea sounded crazy to me, but I thought I better check it out. I sent some samples to a private lab for investigation. The results came back today. Of the twelve samples I sent, four were positive. Two of the four positive samples showed high levels of PCB contamination. There is a real chance that people using the site could come into contact with PCBs.

Alan: (stunned) I can't believe it...You say your results indicate only a "chance" of a threat to public health?

Morena: Well, yes...but do we want to risk it? I think we should postpone the opening of the site and run some more tests.

Alan: There's no need to cause a panic. If this gets out, we'll all be in big trouble. Besides, we can't delay the opening. The whole province is counting on the economic impact of Expo. We have to go ahead with this, despite the risk.

ISSUES

– Is Alan justified in allowing Expo to open on schedule?

– How does one go about deciding what level of risk it is acceptable to take with the public?

– Could you just compare the potential costs in health terms with the benefits to the economy?

– How do you balance the rights of those affected by such a decision?

– What role should "informed consent" play in this calculation?

greatest amount. This approach is similar to the utilitarian ethical theory explained in chapter 1 which requires a determination of "which course of action has the maximum net benefits (or the minimum net costs) for the relevant stakeholders – that is, *everyone* who is significantly affected by it."

The cost-benefit approach to discerning the public interest requires that the interests who are affected by a policy should assign the values to the various policy options. However, since it is not always possible for a policy analyst to consult all affected interests, he or she is often required to make decisions about the values held by these interests even though in practice it is often difficult to discover and measure these values.

Even the advocates of cost-benefit analysis acknowledge the technique's methodological and measurement problems and it is not wise, therefore, to rely solely on this approach to determine where the public interest lies. Nevertheless, the technique is valuable in stimulating thought about alternative ways of achieving government objectives and about the possible consequences of various decisions. It is especially useful for lower-level decisions such as where a post office should be built once a decision has been taken to build it. It is less useful for decisions such as whether the public interest is best served by spending money on a post office or on improved health care. At this level, there is more room for conflicting values which cannot easily be expressed or quantified.

The cost-benefit approach emphasizes the importance of the values of those affected by a decision; yet there are serious objections to interpreting the public interest as the sum of individual interests. In the context of a discussion of the cost-benefit approach to the public interest, Mark H. Moore concludes that "the simple summation of individual preferences attached to effects fails to guide policy because it ignores legitimate *social*, as opposed to individual, values, and the distribution of gains and losses among individuals in different social positions."[21] Would a cost-benefit approach show the way to the right decision in any of the three cases contained in this chapter?

The implications of the cost-benefit route to the public interest can be illuminated by an examination of risk assessment or risk-benefit analysis. Public servants regularly make judgments as to the degree of risk they should take with the public. Many decisions involving risk to the public are easy to make but others are complex and have significant consequences. Risk to the public is involved in such decisions as whether a prisoner should be paroled, how stringent to make regulations on the transport of hazardous products, how vigorously to enforce regulations on the use of pesticides, and what to recommend to political superiors as a trade-off between expenditures on prison guards and police officers on the beat.

It is enlightening to consider risk-benefit analysis in the stark context of assessing what a human life is worth. A.R. Dobell notes that "[a] utilitarian would argue that to maximize total benefit we must assign an appropriate value to a life and take all measures available to save lives at less than this cost. But perhaps not all lives should be valued equally; perhaps the lives that are most at risk should be valued highest."[22]   Eike-Henner Kluge, taking the deonotological perspective, contends that "all other things being equal, decisions that maximize the quality of life of a population at the expense of the life of some of its members are ethically unacceptable even though the number of lives involved be small. Considerations of 'acceptable' losses . . . must be rejected as violating a fundamental right."[23]   How useful are the utilitarian and deontological perspectives in analyzing case 2.2?

Neutral Service and Avoidance of Self-Interest

The four approaches examined above are derived directly from theoretical writings on the public interest. In addition to the practical advice flowing from these approaches, two other considerations should be kept in mind. The first is the importance of neutral service; the second is the avoidance of self-interest.

Neutral Service

As explained earlier, the ethic of neutrality suggests that the public interest is the business of the democratically elected political authorities, not of public servants. However, we have seen that public servants necessarily exercise power in the policy process and make judgments as to what the public interest requires in particular situations. Moreover, only a small proportion of decisions as to the content of the public interest can in practice be taken by political authorities. Under these circumstances, public servants are respon-sible for ensuring that ministers have the necessary information on the implications of policy decisions, including technical and financial implications, which the minister needs to weigh against partisan and short-term considerations. Thus, it can be argued that public servants have an ethical as well as a legal or hierarchical obligation to contribute to the determination of the public interest.

CASE 2.3
THE REAL ISSUE

This conversation takes place between a cabinet minister and Dave, his assistant deputy minister for policy.

Minister: My chief of staff raised the issue of this new women's group – REAL women, isn't that what they're called? They've applied for a grant. Do you think they're a good candidate for federal funding?

Dave: No, I really don't think we ought to take them seriously, Minister. They're a radical fringe whose ideas are totally regressive. They want to see Canadian women barefoot and pregnant in the kitchen.

Minister: Do they have much support? They've been getting a lot of press coverage recently.

Dave: No, they don't have much support at all. You know how the press loves a story like that. It sells newspapers.

Minister: Well, if you really don't think they have a legitimate claim, we'll forget about them.

Dave: I think that's the best idea. The group will probably have disbanded in another year or so.

ISSUES

– Isn't Dave effectively determining that it is not in the public interest to support REAL women? How does he go about achieving that end? What tools does he have at his disposal?

– Would you handle this situation the way Dave did? Would you have "calculated" the social significance of REAL women in the same way?

– Through their discretionary powers as advisers, program managers, and regulators, don't public servants often find themselves in this role?

– Can this discretionary power be handled in such a way that determinations of what is in the public interest do not end up in the hands of public servants?

The public servant who values neutral service highly is likely to emphasize *accountability* to hierarchical superiors so that his or her decisions will reflect the values of political authorities. Before making recommendations and decisions, this public servant will ask such questions as: Have I presented the options fairly and objectively to my superior? Does my advice reflect unduly my personal values? What does my superior want me to do in this case? What would my superior want me to do if he or she knew what I was doing? Case 2.3 demonstrates the power of public servants to dictate the public interest by influencing who gets access to federal funding. Do considerations of neutral service provide useful guidance in this case?

There is a danger that the public interest will not be well served by slavish devotion to neutral service. As explained earlier, public servants are unavoidably involved in making value choices; thus, they can go beyond mere accountability to engage in a more active pursuit of the public interest, both with respect to their own decisions and those of their superiors. This notion is implicit in the advice of the Statement of Principles of the Institute of Public Administration of Canada which states that "public employees should seek to serve the public interest by upholding both the letter *and the spirit* of the laws . . . and of the regulations and directions made pursuant to these laws."

Avoidance of Self-Interest

It is naive to expect that most public servants will be motivated most of the time entirely, or even largely, by selfless considerations. Anthony Downs contends that "every official acts at least partly in his own self-interest, and some officials are motivated solely by their own self-interest."[24] The challenge is to ensure that the reconciliation of competing values in the light of the public interest is not based unduly on self-interest.

Admittedly the public interest is often difficult to discern, but it can usually be distinguished fairly easily, either instinctively or upon reflection, from self-interest. Certain kinds of self-serving behaviour, for example the use of public office for private gain, are readily recognized as contrary to the public interest. Other manifestations of self-interest, for example actions based primarily on considerations of career advancement, are less tangible. To avoid decisions based unduly on self-interest, public servants are encouraged to ask: What is my personal or private interest in this particular decision-making context? As noted earlier, the IPAC Statement of Principles suggests that "public employees should resolve any conflict between their personal or private interests and their official duties in favour of the public interest." Consider the extent to which self-interest is a legitimate consideration in case 2.1.

Public servants make many decisions, ostensibly in the public interest, with which segments of the public disagree. Members of the public are more likely to view these decisions as legitimate if they are convinced that public servants are largely free from self-serving behaviour. To what extent are the public servants in the three cases acting in their self-interest rather than in the public interest?

The Search for a Synthesis

While many of the decisions which public servants make do not give rise to value conflicts, many other decisions involve a conscious choice among competing values in terms of what the public interest requires. None of the approaches discussed above has received general acceptance as an operational guide to determining the public interest. Yet each approach provides useful insights into the elements necessary for such a guide.

First, it is clear that no single value is likely to win universal agreement as the ultimate criterion for determining the public interest. Thus, public servants will normally be required to seek an accommodation of competing values. They should strive, therefore, to articulate and reconcile whatever social, political, administrative, personal, or other values are relevant to the decision. They must be especially mindful of their own dominant values – and of their self-interest – so that their personal values do not overwhelm all other values.

Secondly, all stakeholders likely to be significantly affected by a decision should be identified and consulted. Competing values should be reconciled according to a broader conception of the public interest than "the outcome of competition among diverse interests." This requires at the very least the consideration and reconciliation of interests beyond those of groups and individuals who are well-represented in the decision-making process. From a deontological perspective, Kluge contends that "whenever the matter is of sufficient gravity that the reasonable and prudent person would want to be consulted, ... the ethical public servant must attempt to involve the public by way of informed consent: by facilitating public awareness and engaging in consultation."[25]

Thirdly, certain standards of procedure must be followed in the process of determining the public interest. Public servants should ensure that the procedures followed in obtaining information and consulting those affected by decisions are fair and open. Donald P. Warwick contends that "although the specific content of the public interest can never be established in any precise fashion, its absence can be noted in undue concessions to special interests and in violations of procedural safeguards designed to protect the public at large."[26]

Finally, public servants should do the most comprehensive analysis of the costs and benefits of various decision alternatives that is possible in the circumstances. The greater the cost or risk to the public, the stronger the argument for a thorough cost-benefit analysis. In the sphere of risk analysis, A.R. Dobell notes two extreme stances that responsible public servants should avoid. The first is to exaggerate "the clarity and certainty of the scientific facts relevant to a decision" so that the best decision seems overwhelmingly obvious. The opposite stance is to exaggerate "the lack of factual knowledge available, asserting that questions of public risk are entirely issues of values, and referring every difficult risk decision to polls or referenda for resolution." He concludes that the senior public servant's responsibility is to reconcile "what the analyst sees as the public interest with what the constituency office feels as public pressure. This requires framing decision problems as clearly as possible, and taking seriously the educational role of the public servant ... But in the final analysis, your responsibility as a public servant is to base your decisions and advice on the normative, scientific analysis of the public interest, not on the public opinion polls."[27]

Conclusion

It is clear that there are close parallels between the search for responsible administrative behaviour examined in chapter 1 and the search for the public interest. As noted earlier in this chapter, the duty to "act in the public interest" is very similar in meaning to the broad admonition to "act responsibly." Public servants who are faced with competing values and who wish to act in the public interest are well advised to ask not only tough utilitarian questions (as, for example, in cost-benefit analysis) but also tough deontological questions "about the alternative courses of action suggested and the relevant rules."[28] Responsible public servants will strive to minimize the negative impact on the rights and livelihood of the individuals affected by their decisions. Where appropriate, those adversely affected should be compensated.

Notes

1. Public Service Commission, *Public Service and Public Interest* (Ottawa: Supply and Services, 1978), pp. 11-12.

2. See Dennis F. Thompson, "The Possibility of Administrative Ethics," *Public Administration Review* 45 (September/October 1985), pp. 555-61.

3. J.E. Hodgetts, "Government Responsiveness to the Public Interest: Has Progress Been Made?" *Canadian Public Administration* 24 (Summer 1981), p. 218.

4. Glendon Schubert, *The Public Interest* (Glencoe, Ill.: The Free Press, 1960), p. 220.

5. See Clarke E. Cochran, "Political Science and the 'Public Interest'," *Journal of Politics* 36 (1974), pp. 330-39.

6. Arthur F. Bentley, as quoted in Glendon A. Schubert Jr., "The 'Public Interest' in Administrative Decision-Making," *American Political Science Review* 51 (June 1957), p. 357. See also Arthur F. Bentley, *The Process of Government* (Bloomington, Ind.: Principia Press, 1949 ed.; first published in 1908). See also David B. Truman, *The Governmental Process* (New York: Alfred A. Knopf, 1951); and Frank J. Sorauf, "The Public Interest Reconsidered," *Journal of Politics* 19 (1957), pp. 616-39.

7. James M. Buchanan and Gordon Tullock, *The Calculus of Consent: Logical Foundations of Constitutional Democracy* (Ann Arbor, Mich.: University of Michigan Press, 1962), p. 11.

8. J. Roland Pennock, "The One and the Many: A Note on the Concept of the Public Interest," in Carl J. Friedrich, ed., *Nomos 5: The Public Interest*, (New York: Atherton Press, 1962), p. 182.

9. Walter Lippmann, *The Public Philosophy* (Boston: Little Brown, 1955), p. 42.

10. C.W. Cassinelli, "The Public Interest in Political Ethics," in Friedrich, ed., *Nomos 5: The Public Interest*, p. 46.

11. Cochran, "Political Science and the 'Public Interest'," p. 330.

12. John Rawls, *A Theory of Justice* (Cambridge, Mass.: Harvard University Press, 1971), p. 302. For a critique of Rawls's analysis, see Brian Barry, *The Liberal Theory of Justice* (Oxford: Clarendon Press, 1973).

13. Rawls, *Theory of Justice*, pp. 14-15.

14. H. George Frederickson, "Toward a New Public Administration" in Frank Marini, ed., *Toward a New Public Administration* (Scranton, Pa.: Chandler, 1971), pp. 311, 314 (emphasis in original). See also H. George Frederickson, *New Public Administration* (University, Alabama: University of Alabama Press, 1980), pp. 31-47.

15. Eugene P. Dvorin and Robert H. Simmons, *From Amoral to Humane Bureaucracy* (San Francisco: Canfield Press, 1972), pp. 55, 61 (emphasis in original).

16. See the examples cited in Kenneth Kernaghan, "The Conscience of the Bureaucrat: Conscience or Constraint?" *Canadian Public Administration* 27 (Winter 1984), pp. 581-83.

17. Schubert, *The Public Interest*, pp. 204, 205 (emphasis in the original). Questions related to the fairness of decision-making procedures are explored further in chapter 5.

18. See, for example, J. Rolland Pennock, "The One and the Many: A Note on the Concept," in Friedrich, ed., *Nomos 5: The Public Interest*, p. 180.

19. Anthony Downs, "The Public Interest: Its Meaning in a Democracy," *Social Research* 29 (Spring 1962), p. 5.

20. Hodgetts, "Government Responsiveness," p. 218.

21. Mark H. Moore, "Realms of Obligation and Virtue" in Joel L. Fleishman et al., *Public Duties: The Moral Obligations of Government Officials* (Cambridge, Mass.: Harvard University Press, 1981), p. 19.

22. A.R. Dobell, "The Public Servant as God: Taking Risks with the Public," *Canadian Public Administration* 29 (Winter 1986), p. 609.

23. Eike-Henner W. Kluge, "What Is a Human Life Worth?" in ibid., p. 621.

24. Anthony Downs, *Inside Bureaucracy* (Boston: Little Brown, 1967), p. 53.

25. Kluge, "What Is a Human Life Worth?", p. 621.

26. Donald P.Warwick, "The Ethics of Administrative Discretion" in Fleishman et al., eds., *Public Duties*, p. 112.

27. Dobell, "The Public Servant as God," p. 617.

28. See ch. 1, p. 34.

Chapter 3

The Politically Neutral
Public Servant

Public servants are regularly advised that they have a duty to be
politically neutral. This duty is included in the Statement of Principles
of the Institute of Public Administration of Canada which provides
that "public employees should be sensitive to the political process and
knowledgeable about the laws and traditions regarding political
neutrality that are applicable to their sphere of employment."[1] But
what does political neutrality mean? What *are* the laws and traditions
which constitute the duty to be politically neutral? Is there general
agreement on what these laws and traditions mean and on their
current relevance? What are the links among merit, patronage, and
political neutrality? Where should the balance be struck between
political rights and political neutrality? What does it mean to be loyal
to the government of the day? Where does one draw the line between
political sensitivity and political partisanship? These are some of the
major questions addressed in this chapter.

Defining the Duty

Political neutrality is a constitutional convention which provides that public servants should avoid activities likely to impair, or to seem to impair, their political impartiality or the political impartiality of the public service. The concept of political neutrality is related to, but narrower than, the ethic of neutrality mentioned in chapters 1 and 2. The ethic of neutrality requires that public servants be neutral not only in the partisan sense but also in the broader sense of leaving as many value choices as possible to elected officials. We have already seen that public servants are unavoidably involved in selecting and reconciling values in the course of giving advice and implementing policy; thus, for the great majority of public servants, *value* neutrality is a fiction. *Political* neutrality, in the sense of non-partisan behaviour by permanent, professional public servants, is not a fiction, but its contemporary meaning is significantly different from its traditional meaning.

The meaning of political neutrality can be explained by reference to the model set out below.[2] This model is an ideal-type[3] in the sense that it outlines the requirements for relations between politicians and bureaucrats that would exist in a truly neutral public service in a Westminster-style government. The major tenets of this model are as follows:

1. Politics and policy are separated from administration; thus politicians make policy decisions, public servants execute these decisions;

2. public servants are appointed and promoted on the basis of merit rather than of party affiliation or contributions;

3. public servants do not engage in partisan political activities;

4. public servants do not express publicly their personal views on government policies or administration;

5. public servants provide forthright and objective advice to their political masters in private and in confidence; in return, political executives protect the anonymity of public servants by publicly accepting responsibility for departmental decisions; and

6. public servants execute policy decisions loyally irrespective of the philosophy and programs of the party in power and regardless of their personal opinions; as a

result, public servants enjoy security of tenure during good behaviour and satisfactory performance.

Several points must be made about this model. First, the various tenets of the convention are interconnected, with the result that a change in one of them (for example, political partisanship) is likely to affect one or more of the others (for example, anonymity). Secondly, political neutrality in this extreme form has never existed in any government. Thirdly, the current practice of governments in Canada is significantly different from what the model requires.

The model shows that the duty to be politically neutral can be broken down into such more specific duties as: appoint and promote only on the basis of merit; be non-partisan; avoid public comment on government policies; preserve your anonymity; be loyal. But the rules on these several duties differ from one government to another. Consider, for example, the varying rules just in the areas of political partisanship and public comment. Alberta's rules on political partisanship provide that, except for restrictions on senior public servants and on soliciting financial contributions, "there is no restriction upon participation in political activity by employees."[4] Newfoundland's rules, however, provide that "no employee shall at any time, engage in any partisan activity for or on behalf of any political party or candidate."[5] In the sphere of public comment, the Manitoba rule is that a public servant may speak or write "on behalf of a candidate or a political party in any election, or by-election" so long as he or she does not disclose confidential information.[6] The Ontario rule, by way of contrast, is that "a civil servant shall not at any time speak in public or express views in writing for distribution to the public on any matter that forms part of the platform of a provincial or federal political party."[7]

The political neutrality rules differ even within a single government. For example, the public comment rule in the Canadian Correctional Service forbids public servants from making "repeated public statements which harshly criticize the Service, the Government of Canada, or the Federal Crown, concerning policies, practices and/or programs."[8] The scope of the equivalent rule in the Department of National Revenue (Customs and Excise) is more narrow; it refers to the "incompatibility of criticism or denunciation with the employment relationship" but only in relation to critical comment on persons or policies *within* the department.[9] Some of the rules are very specific but others are subject to considerable interpretation. Several provincial governments (for example, Saskatchewan and Prince Edward Island) provide by statute that no public servants shall at any time take such part in political activities as to impair their usefulness in the position in which they are employed. To what extent is this general prohibition likely to have a chilling effect on the exercise of permissible political activities? Even when such statutory provisions are elaborated by regulations or guidelines, it is often unclear as to precisely what political activities are permissible.

The political neutrality model outlined above applies primarily to federal and provincial governments which, unlike municipal governments, are based on the Westminster model. There is, however, a strong tradition of political neutrality in the municipal sphere of government where municipal employees, like their federal and provincial counterparts, face uncertainties as to the meaning and application of the rules. It is notable also, as explained later in this chapter, that courts in different provinces and courts at different levels in the federal sphere have come to different conclusions about the appropriate balance between political neutrality and political partisanship.

The debate over what the duty to be politically neutral means – and should mean – reflects the fact that there are persuasive arguments for and against political neutrality. Those who are primarily concerned with preserving political neutrality in roughly its existing form note its central place in the Canadian understanding of the Westminster model and its intimate links with the constitutional conventions of ministerial responsibility and public service anonymity. They also point to its importance in ensuring public service appointments and promotions according to merit and in fostering fair and impartial service to the public.

Others believe that existing rules and traditions on political neutrality are too restrictive. They note that undue emphasis on political neutrality suppresses individual rights (notably political rights). They assert also that many current interpretations of the duty to be politically neutral are outdated and unrealistic because relations among politicians, public servants and the public have changed, and continue to change. The examination in this chapter of the components of the political neutrality model provides evidence for both sides of this debate. The first component of the model is not considered here because we have already seen in chapters 1 and 2 that politics, policy, and administration are closely intertwined and that both politicians and public servants are involved in both policy making and policy implementation.

The Meritorious Public Servant

A brief account of the origins and evolution of political neutrality is an essential basis for understanding its links to the issues of merit and patronage. The convention of political neutrality has been a central feature of the constitution since Confederation.[10] The British North America Act of 1867 provided that the Canadian constitution would be "similar in Principle to that of the United Kingdom." Thus, the machinery of Canadian government was organized according to the Westminster model. "There was a convention of political neutrality of Crown servants at the time of Confederation and the reasoning in support of such convention has been consistent throughout the subsequent years." Moreover, "the political neutrality or impartiality of Crown servants is a necessary and fundamental doctrine of the Canadian Constitution, adopted from the Constitution of the United Kingdom."[11]

The practice of political patronage in both Britain and the United States significantly influenced its practice in Canada. "The early British tradition of placing friends in office, which was introduced [into Canada] by the colonial governors, was loyally carried out, and it was even improved upon by adding to it the contemporary American idea that 'to the victor belong the spoils of the enemy.' "[12] Canada did not go so far as to adopt the American spoils system by replacing virtually all public servants when the government changed, but many public servants were appointed on the basis of contributions to the governing party and were replaced when a new government took office.

Political patronage remained a severe obstacle to achieving merit in the public service until 1918 when moral objections to the evils of patronage, combined with the need for greater government efficiency, resulted in major reforms of the public service. Competitive examinations were introduced and the partisan political activities of public servants were severely restricted. Despite these reforms, a large number of patronage appointments continued to be made because many public service positions were exempted from statutory prohibition. The number of patronage appointments gradually diminished over the next several decades and by the 1960s it was generally agreed that patronage in the federal sphere was no longer a serious problem. Provincial governments gradually followed the federal lead by introducing a merit system to promote efficiency and discourage patronage. It is a fact of political life in Canada, however, that patronage appointments continue to be made and that the nature and extent of the practice varies from one government to another.[13]

Many instances or allegations of patronage appointments are reported in the press. But the issue is not so much the number of appointments but the level and type of government posts that are filled by this means. In terms of sheer numbers, appointments at the lower levels of the public service exceed those at the senior levels. In some provinces, where most full-time, permanent positions are filled through a merit system, cabinet ministers make many appointments to temporary and seasonal jobs. In this context, a provincial minister was reported to have said: "Without fail, I will say that the person who worked for me, his son or daughter, has a better chance of getting a (government) job than the person who worked against me. That's a natural instinct of a human being."[14] In terms of influence on the content and administration of public policy, patronage appointments to the senior echelons of the service are much more important. However, both the public and public servants become more agitated over patronage appointments to senior positions in central agencies and operational departments than over appointments to crown agencies. Most governments have tended to restrict patronage appointments to the boards and senior management of crown agencies.

As explained in the next section, one reason given for continuing restrictions on partisan political activity is the desire to avoid a resurgence of patronage. Despite the existence of well-entrenched merit systems, there is continuing concern that the career prospects of public servants will be influenced by their involvement in high-profile partisan politics. It is recognized that merit systems cannot eliminate the covert application of partisan considerations in appointments and promotions. Given the dominant role of public servants in managing the personnel process in general and the merit system in particular, it is important to remember that the duty to be politically neutral requires that public servants make appointments and promotions "on the basis of merit rather than party affiliation or contributions." According to this duty, considerations of partisanship, like those of religion and other criteria unrelated to fitness for the job, should be excluded from hiring and promotion decisions.

The Public Servant's Political Rights

The utilitarian and deontological ethical theories explained in chapter 1 help to clarify the important questions about the relationship between political neutrality and political rights, but they do not provide easy answers to the search for the appropriate balance between these contending values. The "rights" perspective of the deontological approach suggests that public servants should enjoy as many political rights as other citizens; this right clashes, however, with another legitimate right – the right of public officials and members of the public to enjoy the reality and the perception of impartial public service. Similarly, the "consequences" perspective of the utilitarian approach draws attention to the need to calculate carefully which course of action does the most good for the most people. The analysis presented in this chapter will show that this calculus is not easy to make. For example, should the benefit of increased political rights for a limited number of public servants outweigh some loss of real or apparent impartial public service for a large number of citizens?

It is clear that neither the value of political neutrality nor the value of political rights is an absolute value; the challenge, therefore, is to find the optimum balance between them. The IPAC Statement of Principles asserts that "public employees should enjoy the fullest possible measure of political rights that is compatible with laws, regulations and conventions designed to preserve the political neutrality of the public service." As a basis for seeking the best possible balance, it is essential to review the arguments for and against the extension of political rights in the light of the requirements of political neutrality.[15] These arguments should then be considered in relation to case 3.1 on political partisanship and case 3.2 on public comment.

The argument most often presented for extending political rights is that public servants should enjoy the same freedoms of speech and association as other citizens. Proponents of this view refer to the fact that these freedoms are guaranteed under section 2 of the Charter of Rights and Freedoms. The other side of this argument is that the present restrictions are reasonable limits in a free and democratic society under section 1 of the Charter. Opinions on this issue range from the view that public servants should enjoy full political rights to the view that these rights should be strictly limited so as to preserve the reality – and the appearance – of a politically neutral public service. With respect to partisan political activity, the Federal Court of Canada (Trial Division) has said that "a public servant in entering the public service must or should realize that the political neutrality required will necessarily result in some curtailment of his or her partisan political activity even if this involves some restriction on freedom of speech or freedom of association. These restrictions should be as few as possible and no more than are necessary to attain the objective of political neutrality."[16]

Another argument for extending the political rights of public servants is that restrictions on these rights deprive the public in general and political parties in particular of valuable information and insights on public affairs. The argument is also made that restrictions on the political rights of public servants limit the involvement in partisan politics of a large percentage of the most educated citizens in the labour force. Moreover, it is argued that these restrictions are artificial in that they only limit public displays of partisanship; they do nothing to reduce the *feelings* of partisanship that public servants may have. Finally, it is suggested that knowledgeable and skilled persons whose talents are needed in government will be unwilling to accept employment in the public service if their political rights are unduly restricted.

The arguments against the expansion of political rights are primarily arguments in favour of political neutrality. The federal Task Force on Conflict of Interest asserted that:

> In a democratic society it is desirable for all citizens to have a voice in the affairs of the State, and for as many as possible to play an active part in public life. Yet the public interest demands the maintenance of political impartiality in the public service and of confidence in that impartiality as an essential part of the structure of government in this country.[17]

Thus, a common argument for restricting political rights is that the participation of public servants in partisan politics or in public comment undermines public confidence in the impartial conduct of the public's business.

Similarly, it is argued that both ministers and members of the opposition need to have confidence in the loyalty and impartiality of public servants; otherwise, ministers will be inclined to make more patronage appointments, especially at the senior levels of the public service, and opposition members, when they form the government, will be inclined to replace these patronage appointees with their own supporters. Indeed, the argument is frequently made that a substantial expansion in the political rights of public servants will lead to an increase in patronage appointments at all levels of the service and that this will undermine the merit system of appointment and advancement and reduce government efficiency and effectiveness. A final concern about the expansion of political rights relates more to political partisanship than to public comment. This is the concern that if public servants are permitted to engage in a wide range of partisan political activities, they are more vulnerable to exploitation by superiors seeking support for a specific political party or candidate. The IPAC Statement of Principles provides that public servants "should not be compelled to engage in partisan political activities or be subject to threats or discrimination for refusing to engage in such activities."

The great majority of persons on both sides of the issue recognize that its resolution lies in an accommodation of these conflicting viewpoints. The Supreme Court has asserted that "freedom of expression is a deep-rooted value in our democratic system of government . . . but it is not an absolute value . . . All important values must be qualified, and balanced against, other important, and often competing values."[18] The real question, then, is not whether there should be limits on the political rights of public servants but what the extent of these limits should be. The task at hand is to provide the fullest possible measure of political rights that is compatible with the maintenance of the political impartiality of the public service. On the basis of these considerations, we shall discuss the appropriate balance first between political neutrality and political partisanship and then between political neutrality and public comment.

The Partisan Public Servant

The term "partisan political activities" includes a broad range of activities from voting to standing for election. These activities can be divided into two categories: *low-profile* activities (e.g., voting, being a member of a political party, attending political meetings); and *high-profile* activities (e.g., soliciting financial contributions, door-to-door canvassing). There is room for debate over the category to which certain activities properly belong. Some people view attendance at political meetings as high-profile activity; others view the solicitation of financial contributions as low-profile activity (see case 3.1).

Rules on the political activity of public servants can be depicted on a continuum running from the extreme position of no restrictions to the other extreme of political sterilization. In Canada there is considerable variation among governments on the limits of permissible political activity but no government's rules fall at either extreme. Indeed, the issue is not whether there should be some restrictions on partisan political activity but rather how permissive or restrictive the rules should be.

In most governments, public servants are permitted to engage in such low-profile activities as attending political meetings and contributing money to support a political candidate or a political party. These activities are generally considered to pose little threat to the preservation of political neutrality. Some governments restrict or prohibit partisan political activities of a high-profile nature (for example, door-to-door canvassing) which are more likely than low-profile activities to undermine the confidence of the public and elected officials in the political neutrality of the public service.

The argument is often made that public servants should have an unrestricted right to engage in partisan politics unless they have policy-making responsibilities or perform sensitive duties in such areas as personnel management or regulation. The argument on the other side is that the cumulative impact of the participation of large numbers of public servants in high-profile partisan politics may undermine the confidence of the public and of elected officials in the impartiality of the public service.

Seeking nomination and election to public office while on leave of absence is a high-profile activity in which most public servants are, nonetheless, permitted to engage.[19] Thus, some public servants, despite public identification with a particular political party, have

---

**CASE 3.1
SECOND-CLASS CITIZENS?**

This conversation takes place between Dave, a federal public servant, and Andrea, a friend who is a candidate in the upcoming federal election.

Andrea: I'd like you to come to work for me as my campaign manager.

Dave: You know my position. I'm a government employee. I can't get involved in a political campaign.

Andrea: I know what you're thinking. But look, you're an engineer. How much influence could you possibly have over government policy-making?

Dave: Absolutely none, granted. But the logic is that if I publicly declare my political loyalties it would appear that I'm less capable of doing my job impartially. And even the appearance of partisanship is unacceptable.

Andrea: Public servants are not second-class citizens, Dave. You have rights and freedoms just like everyone else. Aren't you going to stand up for yourself?

Dave: I can't, Andrea. I knew what I was doing when I took this job. I knew I would have to make some concessions. I can contribute to your campaign, but I just can't work on it.

ISSUES

– Is it justifiable for Dave's rights as a private citizen to be curtailed in this way because of his employment in the public sector?

– What are the downside risks to the public service of allowing political activity among public servants?

– What is the appropriate extent of political activity for a public servant?

– Are concerns about impartiality with respect to advice and service delivery relevant to an engineer? Might whole groups in the public service be safely allowed more political rights?

---

been reinstated in the public service after losing a bid for nomination or election. Is it consistent to permit the return of public servants involved in such a high-profile political activity while restricting the political activity of public servants involved in less visible activities? Or is the leave of absence and reinstatement policy justified by the

small number of public servants involved and by the undesirability of
the alternative – an absolute prohibition on the right of public servants
to seek political office?

Some of the major concerns about the overt partisan affiliation of
public servants and its effect on loyalty and on the merit system have
been succinctly summarized as follows:

> If a Minister began to consider whether A, on account of his
> party views, might be more capable of carrying out his
> policy than B, the usefulness of B would be limited and the
> opportunities of A would be unfairly improved. This would
> become known, and a tendency to trim the sails to the
> prevailing wind would be one consequence. Another would
> be cynicism about the reasons for promotion very damaging
> to morale ... The danger ... may result from only small
> beginnings, but once begun, it produces a snowball effect,
> which is difficult, if not impossible, to check. Once a doubt is
> cast upon the loyalty of certain individuals or upon the
> equity of the promotion machinery, an atmosphere of
> distrust may rapidly pervade an office and affect the
> arrangement of the work and damage the efficiency of the
> organization.[20]

Many of those who wish to extend the range of permissible
political activity recommend the adoption or adaptation in Canada of
the British regime for regulating political activities.[21] In Britain all
government employees are divided for purposes of political activity
into three categories. A *politically free* group composed of employees at
the lower levels of government service is allowed to take part in a full
range of political activities; an *intermediate* group made up of middle-
level employees is permitted, subject to a code of discretion, to engage
in certain, mostly low-profile, activities; and a *politically restricted*
group composed of higher public servants is prohibited from participating in political activities. This arrangement allows a large number
of public servants to engage actively in partisan politics on the grounds
that they do not hold important policy-making or sensitive posts and
would not, therefore, undermine the public's perception of the
neutrality of the public service.

Some recent actions by Canadian courts and legislatures have
extended the permissible political activities of public servants while
other actions have maintained the status quo. In June 1986 the Nova
Scotia Supreme Court struck down as unduly restrictive the political

activity sections of that province's Civil Service Act.[22] The provincial government responded with new legislation which is somewhat less restrictive than the old legislation but still more restrictive than the rules in most other governments in the country. Then in August 1986 the Trial Division of the Federal Court of Canada made a modest extension to the permissible political activities of federal public servants; in essence, however, the court upheld section 32 (the political activity section) of the federal Public Service Employment Act as compatible with the Charter of Rights and Freedoms because of the importance of the tradition of political neutrality.[23] This decision was overturned in July 1988 by the Federal Court of Appeal which decided that under the Charter section 32 "does not impose a reasonable limit on the freedom of expression and association of federal public servants."[24]   This decision has since been appealed to the Supreme Court of Canada.   However, in August 1988 the federal government responded to the Court of Appeal's decision by introducing Bill C-157, an amendment to the Public Service Employment Act which, compared to the former section 32, greatly extended the political rights of public servants. This bill died on the order paper when the 1988 general election was called.   Finally, the Ontario Supreme Court upheld the political activity sections of the province's Public Service Act, largely on the ground that eliminating the restrictions would lead either to a politicization of the public service or weaken public confidence in its impartiality or independence.[25]

This division of opinion among judges and politicians reflects that among public servants, scholars, and journalists. But at least the extent of disagreement as to what public servants can legally do in this area has been reduced. It is important to ask, however, whether it is sufficient for the responsible public servant simply to adhere to the law or the written rules. Should public servants look to the spirit as well as the letter of the law? The IPAC Statement of Principles notes that "public employees should seek to serve the public interest by upholding both the letter and the spirit of the laws." Surely it is possible to act legally while acting unethically. Take the example of a welfare case worker who during the evening engages legally in door-to-door canvassing for votes in the same neighbourhoods where he or she visits clients during the day.   Or consider the example of an administrative superior who pressures subordinates to work for a specific political party. In some jurisdictions, such coercion is illegal but other jurisdictions have no formal rules on this issue. Is it reasonable to expect public servants to ask themselves not only whether an action is legal but also whether it is ethical?

The Silent Servant

The traditional duty of public servants to be politically neutral requires that they not engage publicly in critical comment on government policies and programs. *Critical* comment needs to be distinguished, however, from the broader concept of *public* comment. Many forms of public comment (for example, the description or explanation of government structures, processes, policies and pro-grams) are acceptable or required activities connected with public servants' formal responsibilities. Beyond these activities are riskier types of public comment such as recommending reforms in government machinery or speculating in public on future government policy. Participation in these activities can occasionally diminish the anonymity or perceived neutrality of the public service.

Then we enter the sphere of public *criticism* which can have significant consequences for anonymity, ministerial responsibility, and political neutrality. The IPAC Statement of Principles provides that "public employees should not express their personal views on matters of political controversy or on government policy or adminis-tration when such comment is likely to impair public confidence in the objective and efficient performance of their duties." At first glance, it may appear crystal clear that public servants cannot with impunity be permitted to criticize government policies or programs. But is it reasonable to forbid public servants to engage in criticism which is unrelated to their official duties or to the policies or programs of their own department? (see case 3.2) What if their comments relate to the policies or programs of another government, for example, comments by a provincial public servant on a federal government policy? What are the circumstances under which public servants should be allowed to engage in public criticism of government?

Some assistance in answering these questions has been provided by the Supreme Court of Canada. The court has stated that "an absolute rule prohibiting all public participation and discussion by all public servants would prohibit activities which no sensible person in a democratic society would want to prohibit." However, "freedom to criticize the Government . . . is not an absolute freedom . . . [W]hereas

---

CASE 3.2
NO COMMENT

The following heated exchange takes place between Paul and Erica, his supervisor, in a federal government department.

Erica: First you send a letter to the editor; next you appear as featured speaker at an anti-metric rally, and now television! Do you have anything to say for yourself before I begin an action to suspend you, Paul?

Paul: Yes, I certainly have. As a Canadian citizen, I have a fundamental right to free speech which is guaranteed by the Charter of Rights and Freedoms. If I don't agree with government policy, I have a right to say so, just like everyone else.

Erica: As a public servant your responsibility is to act with professionalism and impartiality.

Paul: Which I have done. My criticism of the government's metric policy is completely unrelated to my work in this department. I am convinced that I have in no way jeopardized my ability to perform my duties.

Erica: On the contrary, your conduct is going to make it difficult for the minister to have confidence in our department; it is likely to undermine public confidence in our government. I must warn you, Paul, that unless you stop your public criticisms of government policy you risk losing your job.

ISSUES

– Whose position would you defend in the above exchange? Why?

– Would you argue that a public servant should give up some freedom of speech as a part of his or her job?

– What are the appropriate boundaries of public comment?

– Is the subject matter of the comment the key issue here?

---

it is obvious that it would not be 'just cause' for a provincial Government to dismiss a provincial clerk who stood in a crowd on a Sunday afternoon to protest provincial day care policies, it is equally obvious that the same Government would have 'just cause' to dismiss the Deputy Minister of Social Services who spoke vigorously against the same policies at the same rally." We have a "tradition surrounding our public service" which "emphasizes the characteristics of impartiality, neutrality, fairness and integrity . . . [E]mployment in the public service involves acceptance of certain restraints.   One of the most important of those restraints is to exercise caution when it comes to making criticisms of Government."[26] Finally, the court noted that "a public servant may actively and publicly express opposition to the policies of a government . . . if, for example, the Government were engaged in illegal acts, or if its policies jeopardized the life, health or safety of the public servant or others, or if the public servant's criticism had no impact on his or her ability to perform effectively the duties of a public servant or on the public perception of that ability."[27] Similar language has been used to describe the practice of whistle-blowing, that is, the exposure of government wrongdoing involving such activities as violations of the law, gross waste of public money, or threats to the public's safety or health.   Since whistle-blowing is normally interpreted as including the use of confidential or privileged information to expose government wrongdoing, a full treatment of the subject is reserved for chapter 4.

Some governments provide clarification of their public comment rules in their policy guidelines on public servants' communications with the public. For example, Ontario public servants are informed that they have "a duty and a responsibility to communicate with the public, including particularly Members of the Legislative Assembly and representatives of the news media."[28] Public discussion of policy is restricted to ministers; public servants are required to limit themselves to communicating factual information and to avoid discussing "advice or recommendations tendered to Ministers" and speculating "about policy deliberations or future policy decisions." Public servants are also advised that if they act "in good faith" under these guidelines, they "will not be considered as having violated their oaths of secrecy."

Since "good faith" is in the eye of the beholder, it is under-standable that public servants should be cautious in making public statements. Common sense suggests that even comment intended as constructive criticism of government may be perceived by political or administrative superiors as grounds for dismissal or other disciplinary action. The IPAC Statement of Principles notes that "it is the responsibility of public employees to seek approval from the appro-priate governmental authority whenever they are uncertain as to the legality or propriety of expressing their personal views." Given the chilling effect on a public servant's behaviour of having to seek approval from superiors, are there any good reasons why governments should not spell out in specific terms the appropriate bounds of public comment? Is this a feasible suggestion? Should there be a mechanism by which public servants can seek advice when they are uncertain as to how far they can go? These several questions can be considered in relation to the concrete situation set out in case 3.2.

The Responsible Minister

We turn now to an examination of the integral links among the constitutional conventions of political neutrality, ministerial responsibility and public service anonymity. Consider first the issue of ministerial responsibility.

There are two schools of thought on the current relevance of the convention (or doctrine) of ministerial responsibility. Some commentators, the *pragmatists*, contend that the doctrine is a myth; others, the *constitutionalists*, view it as a key doctrine of our cabinet-parliamentary form of government.[29] This is an important difference of perspective because if ministers cannot be held responsible, the burden of responsibility shifts to public servants. Before examining these contending views, it is important to explain the traditional doctrine of ministerial responsibility since disagreement about its relevance is based in part on confusion about its meaning.[30]

A distinction must be made between collective and individual ministerial responsibility. *Collective* ministerial responsibility, or cabinet responsibility as it is often called, refers to the requirement that the cabinet as a whole answer to the legislature for the content and administration of government policies. The cabinet must resign if it loses a vote of confidence in the legislature. Disagreements among cabinet ministers must be expressed within the confines of the cabinet room, not in public, and ministers who find it necessary to criticize government policy publicly must resign.

The doctrine of *individual* ministerial responsibility has two principal requirements. First, it requires that ministers answer to the legislature for everything that happens within their department so that if a significant mistake is made the minister must resign. Secondly, it requires that ministers answer to the legislature in the sense of explaining and defending all departmental actions. The corollary of these requirements is that public servants do not answer directly to the legislature. According to the Westminster model, public servants are accountable to their ministers, not to the legislature.

Some of the pragmatists ignore or downplay the second element of ministerial responsibility; thus, they claim that since ministers do not meet the first requirement by resigning in the event of serious departmental error, the doctrine is a myth. Even those pragmatists who do recognize the second element as an integral part of the doctrine argue that ministers are not in practice held effectively answerable by this method.

The constitutionalists deny that the doctrine of ministerial responsibility is a myth. Indeed, they view it as a central feature of the Canadian constitution in that it focuses responsibility for departmental actions on an individual minister in the same fashion as collective ministerial responsibility focuses responsibility on the cabinet. They agree with the pragmatists that ministers cannot reasonably be expected to resign over departmental errors about which they had no personal knowledge and they recognize the difficulty of securing ministerial resignations for errors even when ministers have such knowledge. The constitutionalists do, however, assert that the second element of ministerial responsibility has considerable vitality in that ministers generally feel bound to explain and justify departmental actions to the legislature; moreover, ministers often pay a political price in the form of demotion or other penalty for performing this responsibility poorly.

The different views on the meaning and application of ministerial responsibility can be effectively represented on a continuum ranging from those pragmatists who argue for a major reformulation of the doctrine to those constitutionalists who argue that all incursions on the operation of the traditional doctrine should be resisted.

Those commentators lying near the pragmatist pole of the continuum are criticized for their inability to devise a viable alternative formulation of the doctrine that respects principles of cabinet-parliamentary government. Most of the proposed reformulations involve a sharing of responsibility between ministers and public servants. Proposals range from a regime where public servants would answer directly to the legislature for specified administrative duties to a regime where public servants would take a public stand on policy issues; in the latter instance, differences of opinion with ministers would be justified by reference to a higher good such as the public interest or individual conscience. Thus, some proposals involve relatively minor departures from the traditional doctrine whereas others verge on a new constitutional order where public servants would have a constitutional *persona* separate from that of their minister. At some point in this range of options, a reformulation of the doctrine of ministerial responsibility becomes a new formulation of relations between ministers and public servants.

To hold pubic servants directly accountable to the legislature for certain designated administrative matters would not be a revolutionary departure from the traditional doctrine.[31] However, to hold public servants directly accountable to the legislature for their policy contributions would have significant effects not only on the doctrine of ministerial responsibility but also on public service anonymity and neutrality. The possible effects have been described as follows:

> Relations between ministers and public servants would be complicated by the difficulty of distinguishing their respective contributions to the development of specific policies. The answerability of public servants to Parliament would compete with their accountability and loyalty to their minister. The remaining healthy component of ministerial responsibility – the answerability of ministers – would be severely weakened . . . There would be a dramatic decline in public service anonymity and the senior echelons of the public service would be politicized. Public servants would be compelled to defend their policy recommendations before parliamentary committees and the public. Officials would become personally associated with particular policies and would, therefore, become involved in political controversy. Security of tenure for senior officials would be replaced by a system of political appointments and a consequent turnover of public servants with a change in government.[32]

This scenario demonstrates well the interdependence of the elements of the model of political neutrality explained earlier.

Those commentators located near the constitutionalist pole of the continuum are considered unrealistic for suggesting a return to the traditional requirements of the doctrine. We shall see that the feasibility of their suggestion depends on developments affecting the conventions of anonymity and political neutrality. It is difficult to bring about ministerial responsibility in its pristine form in the face of significant modifications to these related conventions.

There is comparatively little disagreement between those constitutionalists and pragmatists who are found toward the middle of the continuum. Many pragmatists recognize that the doctrine fulfills a useful normative purpose and many constitutionalists admit that the current operation of the doctrine departs somewhat from its traditional requirements. However, the departures to date do not appear to be extensive enough to alter significantly the loyalty requirement of political neutrality. Can the same be said of the convention of public service anonymity?

The Anonymous Public Servant

The traditional model of political neutrality requires that the responsible minister be complemented by the anonymous public servant. Ministers are expected to take public credit and public blame for departmental actions so as to protect the anonymity of their officials. Public servants are expected to protect their own anonymity by providing frank and impartial advice to ministers in private and in confidence and by refraining from activities which will involve them – or appear to involve them – in partisan politics. Like the conventions of political neutrality and ministerial responsibility, however, public service anonymity has in practice been somewhat eroded. Is the duty of anonymity still a useful and realistic one?

Public servants receive conflicting signals as to the current meaning of public service anonymity. In general, they are expected to preserve their anonymity but at the same time they are required to perform tasks which undermine their anonymity. In support of their ministers, they now appear regularly before legislative committees where their policy views and policy contributions sometimes become evident. Moreover, increased emphasis on public participation in government decision-making has brought more public servants into direct and frequent contact with members of the public, either in public forums or in private offices. The policy influence of public servants is often evident also during their consultations and negotiations on behalf of their ministers with pressure group representatives. The higher visibility of public servants resulting from the combined impact of these developments is compounded by the increased focus of the news media on the activities and influence of public servants.

It has been suggested also that freedom of information legislation recently enacted by several governments is likely to erode public service anonymity because more documentary information on the decisions and recommendations of public servants will become available. An offsetting consideration, however, is that the names of the public servants involved are usually blacked out on such documents. In addition, most of the politically sensitive material is excluded from disclosure.

Ministers differ in the importance they attach to public service anonymity and to the traditional requirements of ministerial responsibility. Some ministers are more inclined than others to permit public servants to interact with legislators, members of the public, pressure group representatives, and the media. A few ministers have gone so far as to identify and criticize publicly officials allegedly guilty of maladministration. Such incidents not only severely strain the doctrine of ministerial responsibility; they also diminish public service morale because public servants, as part of their commitment to anonymity – and to keeping their jobs, cannot usually respond publicly to such allegations.

Part of the burden for retaining anonymity rests with the public servants themselves. Gordon Robertson, a former secretary to the federal cabinet, has argued that "anonymity ... involves a substantial act of self-denial. It means an unwillingness to hint at influential association with policies or decisions; refusal to give the private briefing of a journalist that can lead to a benevolent and admiring story; avoidance of photographs with the great; and, within reasonable limits, eschewing the physical trappings of status that are demonstrations to the beholder of unspoken power and importance."[33] However, the current role of public servants in the political process often brings them into the public spotlight. The convention of ministerial responsibility provides some direction in that it still requires that they limit their public activities to *explaining* government policies, while leaving ministers to *defend* these policies. When public servants drift over the sometimes indistinguishable line between the explanation and the defence of policy, they may be perceived as having entered the partisan political arena. In this context, their comments and identities will receive much greater publicity.

What should public servants do if obeying their minister's (or their administrative superior's) instructions will involve them in activities which will significantly diminish their anonymity? Should they resist the instructions only if the activities would involve them (or appear to involve them) in partisan politics? Can they justify their resistance on the grounds of ministerial responsibility and political neutrality? Does loyalty to the minister and the government of the day override considerations of anonymity?

The Loyal Public Servant

Traditionally, security of tenure for public servants has required that they serve loyally and impartially whatever political party is in power. In return, they have been assured of security of tenure during good behaviour and satisfactory performance. Yet recent changes of government in both the federal and provincial spheres have resulted in the dismissal of senior public servants who were alleged to be patronage appointees and in their replacement with friends of the governing party. In the federal government, most of the dismissals and new appointments involved agencies, boards, and commissions rather than regular government departments. However, the election of the Conservative government in Saskatchewan in 1982 led to the removal of a large number of career public servants in regular departments. Moreover, many of those dismissed to make room for supporters of the new government had no affiliation with any political party.

The preference of ministers as between a permanent and a politicized senior public service will depend greatly on their confidence in the loyalty of public servants. But what does the loyalty of the public servant mean in this context? Does it mean the same thing to ministers as to public servants? How does the public servant walk the narrow line between sensitivity and partisanship?[34]

The IPAC Statement of Principles provides that "public employees have a duty to carry out government decisions loyally, irrespective of the party or persons in power and irrespective of their personal opinions." Thus, public servants are expected to serve successive governments with equal loyalty. They are, in short, expected to be political chameleons whose colour changes with a change in the political complexion of the governing party. Loyalty does not mean that public servants are neutral as between the government and the opposition; rather it means that they are non-partisan. They are, nevertheless, expected to apprise their minister of the political consequences of pursuing various courses of action. They are expected to be politically sensitive rather than politically partisan. The difficulty of discerning the appropriate line between political sensitivity and political partisanship is demonstrated in case 3.3.

Does loyalty to the government mean the same thing as loyalty to the government of the day? Two former secretaries to the federal cabinet have had an illuminating exchange of views on this issue. Michael Pitfield asserted that there is "a large element of truth" in the argument that permanent officials have a duty "by legal and proper means, to keep in power the Government that the legal process has given them until such time as it gives them another." Moreover, "it is the duty of the permanent public service to support the government in power."[35] Gordon Robertson responded with the contention that "it is dangerous . . . to suggest that a public servant has any 'duty' to promote that 'staying in power' or to generalize the proposition about providing good advice into a duty 'to support the government in power'." Further, "the senior public servant is entitled to have his own political beliefs . . . However, he has neither the duty nor the right to have as his purpose and objective the maintenance in power of a government simply because it happens, by legal process, to be there – or because he happens, in his personal opinions, to favour its policies."[36] This view has been supported by the Supreme Court of Canada in its declaration that "as a general rule, federal public servants should be loyal to their employer . . . The loyalty owed is to the Government of Canada, not the political party in power at any one time . . . [T]here is a powerful reason for this general requirement of loyalty, namely, the public interest in both the actual, and apparent, impartiality of the public service."[37]

It does not follow that loyalty to the government as opposed to the government of the day requires blind loyalty. As explained in chapter 2, public servants may believe that their ultimate loyalty (or responsibility) is not to the government but to the public, to the public interest, or to their own conscience. Are public servants bound to obey governments or ministers who act outside the law or who take decisions that the public servant's conscience cannot bear? Surely the answer must be no, but for their own sake public servants must be sure of their ground before they disobey their minister's instructions. The IPAC Statement of Principles asserts that "it is the responsibility of public employees to provide forthright and objective advice to, and carry out the directions of, their political superiors." This principle

CASE 3.3
DRAWING THE LINE

A conversation is overheard between two public servants.

Donna: The minister's going to love this program. It'll be very popular and will undoubtedly increase the government's standing in the polls. It will also make the department look very good.

Martin: It's not our job to make the government look good. Our concern should extend only so far as to give the best advice possible. You shouldn't be concerned about the political implications of your advice.

Donna: Well, that goes with the territory. We work closely with politicians in devising policy. If we do a good job, the government looks good. That's the way it is. We work for political masters.

Martin: You're going too far, Donna! Not every policy that is advisable is going to be politically popular. Public servants who become fixated by the popularity of the government are ignoring their professional responsibilities.

Donna: You're exaggerating, Martin. The public service must help the government make good decisions. An essential component of policy-making is political feasibility. In that sense, I suppose you could say that the public servant must support the party in power. That's what we're here for.

Martin: Yes, but there's a fine line between political sensitivity and political partisanship, and you've stepped over it.

ISSUES

– Whose side would you take in this debate, Donna's or Martin's?

– Does the public servant's duty of loyalty to the minister mean that he or she should do anything required to keep the minister out of trouble and the government in power?

– Is there a line between political sensitivity and political partisanship? How would you characterize it?

– Is the kind of public service Donna seems to support a politically neutral public service?

must sometimes be interpreted in the light of the assertion in the Statement's preamble that "on occasion difficult decisions facing public employees can ultimately be resolved only by resorting to individual conscience."

Conclusion

The policies and practices of governments in Canada vary significantly from the requirements of the idealized model of political neutrality explained earlier in this chapter.[38] The extent of this variation differs from one government to another and even from one department to another within a single government. Moreover, not only public servants but judges, legislators, journalists, and academics as well are uncertain or in disagreement as to the current meaning of the public servant's duty to be politically neutral. The task of defining this duty is complicated by the fact that some of the rules bearing on political neutrality, notably those affecting political rights, are in a state of flux.

The constitutional convention of political neutrality and the related conventions of ministerial responsibility and public service anonymity are central to the operation of the political system in general and the public service in particular. But has too much emphasis been placed on preserving these conventions in their traditional form? Are further departures from the various components of political neutrality desirable or feasible? Our examination of the issues surrounding each of these components should assist the reader to determine what measure of political neutrality is compatible with responsible public service.

Notes

1. Institute of Public Administration of Canada, *Statement of Principles Regarding the Conduct of Public Employees* (Toronto: Institute of Public Administration of Canada, 1986). See Appendix.

2. For elaboration on this model, see Kenneth Kernaghan, "Politics, Policy and Public Servants: Political Neutrality Revisited," *Canadian Public Administration* 19 (Fall 1976), pp. 432-56.

3. An ideal type is a theoretical tool which simplifies reality so as to provide conceptual clarity. The closer a government comes to achieving the requirements of the model, the closer it is to achieving political neutrality in an absolute sense.

4. Alberta, "Code of Conduct and Ethics for the Public Service of Alberta," sec. 5.

5. Newfoundland, Order-in-Council 951-75, August 18, 1975.

6. Manitoba, Civil Service Act, Revised Statutes of Manitoba, 1970, c-110, as amended by Statutes of Manitoba, 1974, c. 46.

7. Ontario, Public Service Act, Revised Statutes of Ontario, 1980, c. 418.

8. Correctional Service of Canada, "Code of Discipline," sec. 19(d).

9. "Customs and Excise Code," sec. 11(d).

10. The evolution of political neutrality in Canada has been greatly affected by developments in Britain and the United States. For a comparative perspective on Britain and the United States, see S.E. Finer, "Patronage and the Public Service," *Public Administration* (London) 30 (1952), pp. 329-60. For a comparative perspective on Britain and Canada, see David E. Smith, "Patronage in Britain and Canada: An Historical Perspective," *Journal of Canadian Studies* 22 (Summer 1987), pp. 34-53.

11. *Re Ontario Public Service Employees Union et al. and Attorney-General for Ontario* (1980), 31 O.R. (2e): 330.

12. R. McGregor Dawson, *The Civil Service of Canada* (London: Oxford University Press, 1929), p. 25.

13. See J.D. Love, "The Merit Principle in Provincial Governments of Atlantic Canada," *Canadian Public Administration* 31 (Fall 1988), pp. 335-51.

14. *Globe and Mail*, June 16, 1986.

15. For a detailed consideration of these competing arguments, see Kenneth Kernaghan, "Political Rights and Political Neutrality: Finding the Balance Point," *Canadian Public Administration* 29 (Winter 1986), pp. 639-52. In the same volume, see Michael Cassidy, "Political Rights for Public Servants: A Federal Perspective (1)," pp. 653-64, and Edgar Gallant, "Political Rights for Public Servants: A Federal Perspective (2)," pp. 665-68.

16. *Randy Barnhart, Linda Camponi, Michael Cassidy, Ken Clavette and Heather Stevens* v. *The Queen,* Court File No. T-163-84, transcript of reasons for judgment dated August 22, 1986, pp. 33-34.

17. Government of Canada, Task Force on Conflict of Interest, *Ethical Conduct in the Public Sector* (Ottawa: Supply and Services, 1984), p. 46.

18. Supreme Court of Canada, *Neil Fraser and Public Service Staff Relations Board* (1985) 2 SCR: 462-63.

19. Between 1967 and 1985, permission was granted to 167 out of 187 federal public servants (about 90 per cent) who requested leave of absence to stand for nomination or election. See the testimony of Edgar Gallant, then chairman of the Public Service Commission, before the Miscellaneous Estimates Committee of the House of Commons, May 21, 1985, pp. 20-21.

20. United Kingdom, *Report of the Committee on the Political Activities of Civil Servants* (Cmd. 7718, 1949), para. 43.

21. For a detailed examination of the British model, see Ontario Law Reform Commission, *Political Activity, Public Comment and Disclosure by Crown Employees* (Ontario: Ministry of the Attorney General, 1986), pp. 165-86.

22. *Re Fraser et al. and Attorney General of Nova Scotia et al.,* 30 DLR (4th): 340-75.

23. *Osborne* v. *The Queen and two other actions* 30 DLR (4th): 662-90.

24. *William James Millar* v. *The Queen,* File No. A-542-86; *Bryan Osborne* v. *The Queen,* File No. A-543-86; and *Randy Barnhart, Linda Camponi, Michael Cassidy, Ken Clavette and Heather Stevens* v. *The Queen,* File No. A-556-86, July 15, 1986, p. 10 of typescript.

25. *Ontario Public Service Employees Union, Wayne Pierce, Christina Schenk, Russell B. Smith, Adriana Nelson and Marilyn Youden* v. *The Attorney General of Ontario,* August 5, 1988.

26. *Neil Fraser and Public Service Staff Relations Board,* pp. 467, 468, 471.

27. Ibid., p. 470.

28. Government of Ontario, *Policy Guidelines for Civil Servants on Communications with the Public,* dated October 3, 1980, and

tabled in the Legislative Assembly on October 9. See *Ont. Leg. Ass., Sessional Papers* 314/215 (October 9, 1980).

29. See V. Seymour Wilson, *Canadian Public Policy and Administration* (Toronto: McGraw-Hill Ryerson, 1981), pp. 196 ff.

30. For a detailed examination of the meaning of ministerial responsibility, see Kenneth Kernaghan, "Power, Parliament and Public Servants in Canada: Ministerial Responsibility Reexamined," *Canadian Public Policy* 3 (Summer 1979), pp. 383-96, and T.M. Denton, "Ministerial Responsibility: A Contemporary Perspective," in R. Schultz et al., eds., *The Canadian Political Process* (Toronto: Holt, Rinehart and Winston, 1979), pp. 344-62.

31. See the discussion of the accountability of deputy ministers in chapter 7.

32. Kernaghan, "Power, Parliament and Public Servants," p. 394.

33. Gordon Robertson, "The Deputies' Anonymous Duty," *Policy Options* 4 (July 1983), p. 13.

34. For a difference of opinion on this issue between two former secretaries to the federal cabinet, see ibid., pp. 12-13.

35. Michael Pitfield, "Politics and Policy Making," address to the Alma Mater Society, Queen's University, Kingston, February 10, 1983, pp. 7, 8.

36. Robertson, "The Deputies' Anonymous Duty," p. 12.

37. Chief Justice Dickson in *Neil Fraser and Public Service Staff Relations Board* (1985), 2 SCR: 470.

38. See Ontario Law Reform Commission, *Political Activity, Public Comment and Disclosure by Crown Employees*, pp. 24-25, which is an expanded version of the statement in Kenneth Kernaghan, "Power, Parliament and Public Servants in Canada," p. 393.

Chapter 4

Confidentiality and Privacy

Virtually all governments require their public servants to safeguard secret and confidential information. The Institute of Public Administration of Canada's Statement of Principles endorses this widely accepted practice when it states that: "Public employees should not disclose to any member of the public, either orally or in writing, any secret or confidential information acquired by virtue of their official position." But the Statement also adds that: "Within the bounds of law and propriety, public employees should be sensitive and responsive to the needs of the public, the news media and legislators for information on and explanations of the content and administration of government policies and programs."

Within and between these two statements lurk difficult dilemmas for the public servant. In a liberal democratic society how does one justify keeping vital information from the public and from other participants in policy-making and administrative processes? Does a public servant have a positive duty to provide information, separate from reactive obligations arising from freedom of information legislation? Is it ever appropriate to mislead the public by providing false or distorted information? Under what conditions is it appropriate or even obligatory to blow the whistle publicly, and to whom should you give the information if you do? What role do traditional claims to privacy play in all of this? What is the nature of the public servant's duty to protect the privacy of citizens and corporations?

Confidentiality and privacy are problem areas in which the intuitions of public servants about how to act in specific situations are often distant from the traditional rules governing their behaviour. This chapter examines what it means to deal responsibly with government information in a society preoccupied by the importance of knowledge.

Confidentiality: Defining the Duty

The duty not to disseminate secret and confidential information obtained in the course of one's work is an obligation recognized and enforced by the common law, oaths of secrecy, the Criminal Code, the Official Secrets Act, non-disclosure provisions of specific statutes, codes of conduct, and occasional special directives by individual governments. While the accumulated case law provides for significant exceptions where there is a public interest in exposure, overall, the common law has established a significant duty of confidentiality on employees.[1] This duty is complemented and recognized more specifically with respect to government employees in the oath of secrecy that they take when joining government service. Most federal, provincial and municipal governments in Canada demand that employees take an oath of office that includes an undertaking to maintain confidentiality.[2] "Leaving aside minor differences of language, in each oath the employee swears not to disclose or make known, without due authorization, any matter or thing that comes to his or her knowledge by reason of employment in the public service."[3]

To this wide-ranging prohibition, public servants must add restrictions on disclosure emanating from the Criminal Code and the Official Secrets Act. The former appears to treat any unauthorized disclosure by a public servant as a breach of trust under Section 111. The latter "makes the wrongful communication of information a criminal offence, punishable under conviction by imprisonment for a term not to exceed fourteen years."[4] Some jurisdictions also use legislation to place more specific restrictions on employees working in certain areas (taxation, immigration, statistics, health records, etc.).

Codes of conduct or special guidelines often further reinforce the non-disclosure duty. The "Code of Conduct for Employees of the Municipality of Metropolitan Toronto," for instance, has four sections devoted to the unauthorized release of information on individual citizens, personnel matters, and matters under negotiation or litigation. The focus throughout these sections is on the need to obtain authorization before releasing any information obtained through employment by the municipality. By contrast, the "Code of Conduct and Ethics for the Public Service of Alberta" refers to confidentiality only briefly in the context of rules about public statements. The code reminds public servants of the obligations flowing from their oath of office and states their responsibility not to allow confidential information to be made directly or indirectly available to unauthorized persons.

Such codes are supplemented in many jurisdictions by guidelines for public servants, issued by the government in response to a crisis or "growing concern" about the information being disseminated by appointed officials. In 1981 the federal government issued a guideline entitled "Briefings by Officials to Parliamentary Caucuses" which limited officials to providing "factual and background material necessary to allow informed consideration of the subject under discussion, consistent with preserving the necessary confidences of government." Beyond that point authorization from a minister would be required and officials were warned not to divulge "information whose disclosure is prohibited by existing law or would otherwise be unethical or unprofessional." Similarly, the Prime Minister's Office issued "Policy Guidelines for Public Servants: Communications with the Public" in 1984. This directive was intended to regulate communications between public servants and the media. Public servants were cautioned only to provide information "that describes or explains programs and policies that have been announced or implemented by the government." Moreover, they were to speak to the media only "on the record and for attribution by name." Off-the-record background briefings would only be permitted "in exceptional circumstances and must have prior Ministerial approval."[5]

On the other side, public servants are confronted with commitments to "open government" by the politicians they serve, and the use of "leaks" by ministers, ministerial staff members, and their bureaucratic superiors. The Freedom of Information and Personal Privacy Act in Ontario removes the threat of civil or criminal actions against public servants who disclose confidential information in good faith.[6] The British Columbia "Standards of Conduct" for public servants goes further, spelling out an obligation to blow the whistle where a law has been broken, public funds misused, or public health and safety endangered.[7]

In some jurisdictions public servants also must contend with a countervailing public right to government information under freedom of information legislation. Such legislation usually creates a reactive duty on the part of the public servant to provide to members of the public the information which they specifically request, subject to a set of exemptions that recognize the opposing concerns about confidentiality.[8] The public servant is generally under no obligation to bring the existence of specific information to the attention of inquiring members of the public. Moreover, the exemptions are usually extensive, closing off access to cabinet confidences, a wide spectrum of information on policy-making and operational planning, information obtained in confidence from other governments, records which could disrupt the conduct of federal-provincial relations, international affairs, and defence, information relating to law enforcement, and a host of other types of data which may injure individuals, groups, or businesses. The relationship between freedom of information legislation on the one hand, and the statutes, regulations, and guidelines enforcing confidentiality on the other, is spelled out in different ways in different jurisdictions, but many legal uncertainties remain.

In fact, ambiguity, *ex post facto* judgments and mixed messages are the trademark of this whole area. In this tug of war between secrecy and openness, public servants cannot be certain about how to interpret their duty not to divulge confidential information. The common law duty of confidentiality has been shot through with exceptions as a result of recent court decisions.[9] Experts regularly insist that the confidentiality obligations of oaths of office have "no basis in law."[10] Gordon Robertson concludes that the federal oath "is unrealistic and it lends itself to ridicule really, and a failure to abide by it because of that."[11] The Official Secrets Act has been condemned as one of the poorest examples of legislative drafting in the statute books. Although this legislation has been little used in recent years, its prohibition of the communication of information is so broad that virtually any unauthorized disclosure could result in criminal liability.[12]

In any case, a public servant rarely knows until after the fact whether the slippery standards of the common law, oaths of office, or official secrets legislation have been violated. Codes of conduct and guidelines generally perpetuate this vague, amorphous approach and do little to reduce the tension between the duty to disclose and the duty of confidentiality. Similarly, specific statutes (e.g., on the management of statistics) tell one what you cannot do, but are silent on what one can or *should* do. Finally, freedom of information legislation provides the public servant with guidelines for "reactive" disclosure but, again, says little about the proactive obligation to disclose information to the public. In short, while the balance of direction is strongly in favour of confidentiality, this congeries of laws and guidelines does not provide the public servant with a standard of behaviour.

For and Against Secrecy

If we exclude, for the moment, considerations related to the protection of privacy, what arguments can be mustered for and against the presumption of secrecy which seems to dominate public administration? Sisela Bok argues that underlying what is, for the most part, a utilitarian approach to the defence of secrecy is an "esoteric rationale" which suggests that secrecy is even more justifiable for governments than it is for individuals; that governments have a right to keep the "secrets of rule" or "mysteries of state" from the people.[13]

Failing the persuasiveness of a doctrine flowing from the divine right of kings, other more results-oriented rationales for secrecy are at hand. In essence, these are arguments rooted in a concern about government's capacity to carry out its role effectively. Secrecy is essential to make and implement plans, to negotiate, and to protect citizens from enemies. The long shadow of these traditional rationales is easily visible in the types of exemptions which are commonplace in contemporary freedom of information legislation.

But let us look at these rationales a little more closely. In Canada and other countries that have adopted the Westminster model of government, the utilitarian concern about the ability to make and implement plans has become intertwined with a constitutional rationale for secrecy. Our system of responsible cabinet government, it is argued, won't work unless cabinets, their committees, ministers and supporting bureaucracies are allowed to develop, discuss, and argue about the widest possible set of policy alternatives before choosing one, sealing the various compromises, closing ranks, and applying the convention of collective ministerial responsibility for that decision. Similarly, as we have discussed in chapter 3, the views and roles of public servants in the decision-making process must be kept dark to protect their anonymity and further buttress the notions of collective and individual ministerial responsibility. As Gordon Robertson so eloquently puts it:

> It has always been recognized as fundamental to the principle of ministerial responsibility for policy that confidentiality be maintained about advice received from officials. It is the Ministers who decide: the policy is theirs. It does not matter whether it was devised by officials, or whether they argued for or against it. The principles would not last long, nor would the anonymity of the public service, if Cabinet documents became publishable without some prescribed and substantial delay.[14]

Of course, the utilitarian justification for secrecy does not draw the line at cabinet documents related to policy development. A strong argument is also made for protecting government capacity to deliver policy. Effectiveness in implementation often calls for stealth which, in turn, depends on secrecy. The details of a criminal investigation cannot be made known to the public without being made known to the criminals. Fairness and equity may also be at stake. The regulatory regime for a new tax policy cannot be displayed prematurely for fear that some crafty citizens will negate the intention of the new taxes. For the same reasons, the decision-making process leading to an adjustment of interest rates or the devaluation of the currency must be kept secret until the government is ready to move.

This logic is easily extended to the whole realm of negotiation. A government cannot bargain successfully with unions, corporations, or other levels of government if its position is widely known. The ultimate realm of secrecy, of course, is information about a government's relationships and negotiations with foreign governments and its preparation for defence or attack. As Sissela Bok points out: "At the root of the rationale for military secrecy is the imperative of self-preservation . . . And because a degree of military secrecy is so fundamental to survival, it can call on greater sacrifices than all other rationales for secrecy."[15] There is nothing like the threat of an outside enemy to buttress a government's argument that even the normal concerns about the intentional concealment of information have to be put aside.

Overall, then, democratic governments argue that to govern effectively they must conceal a good deal of information from the citizens they represent. Thus public servants are confronted with a strong message to keep their mouths shut and their file drawers locked unless otherwise instructed. But what about the arguments on the other side? What kind of case can be made for a presumption of disclosure rather than secrecy?

The most telling argument against secrecy in a democratic society is its impact on the distribution of power. Secrecy gives power to those who hold the information and removes it from the uninformed. Without information, citizens lose their capacity to both influence public policy-making and scrutinize the actions of government. Widespread participation and accountability are both essential features of a healthy democracy. Donald Smiley argues that "information must be so distributed that public debate is not a 'dialogue of the deaf' between those who don't know and those who won't tell."[16] In recent years there has been an increasing tendency to see timely access to government information as a basic right of a citizen in a democratic society.[17]

The relationship between information and meaningful participation is obvious and goes well beyond concern for creating an informed electorate ready to cast their ballots intelligently. Groups or individual members of the public who are immediately affected or merely concerned about the development of government policy in a particular area are in no position to join the debate and argue their case persuasively if they do not have access to the array of information which the government has gathered to support its proposals.

While a "rights" (or deontological) perspective on information-sharing may be a good place to start, there are parallel "consequence" (or utilitarian) arguments which are equally powerful. Providing the information required for citizens and groups to participate in the decision-making process in the planning stage reduces the distrust of government and increases its efficiency. The Ontario Commission on Freedom of Information and Privacy argued that:

> ... the effect of public awareness of and participation in decision-making processes may reduce the intensity of protracted public debate concerning proposed government initiatives. It is simply inefficient for governments to make decisions and to devote considerable resources to the development of programs only to have them subsequently either rejected by an angry public or subjected to the expense and delay of prolonged reconsideration and inquiry.[18]

Our contemporary approach to policy-making is one in which groups and individuals make mutual adjustments in order to achieve as much of their desired ends as possible. "What makes mutual adjustment work is the wide availability of relevant information, so each mutual adjuster can figure out what the others might do under varied conditions and give forth useful signals about his or her own behaviour."[19] In short, the benefits of making more information available considerably outweigh the costs.

Similarly, the accountability of government officials for actions taken cannot survive and prosper without the free flow of information between government and its citizens. Secrecy means that individuals and institutions that have a right within our model of responsible democratic government to scrutinize the performance of government often lack the information required to even formulate relevant questions. A citizen or a legislative committee cannot examine government actions if data about the implementation of policy are withheld or only made available when specifically requested. Despite the traditional focus of accountability on elected officials, this concern is perhaps even more relevant to public administrators than politicians. It is the former who breathe life into the policy decisions of the latter and it is the identification of those who exercise discretionary authority under legislation and knowledge about how they exercise that authority that are the key building blocks of an administrative accountability regime.

A system that fosters confidentiality about the operation of government might also be fostering abuse of administrative power. In any case, it is clearly the public perception – reinforced by the media – that a government which is unduly secretive must have something to hide. That something is, as often as not, incidents of waste of resources, negligence with respect to the health or safety of the public, conflicts of interest, or misdirection of funds.

There are a number of consequentialist arguments in favour of greater openness which are not directly related to the democratic values of participation and accountability. David Curzon argues that secrecy can endanger the efficacy of the decision-making process in government.[20] Keeping information within a small circle of decision-makers and advisers can hide the fact that the premises upon which a decision is based are simplistic or biased. If the premises are faulty, then the decision is unlikely to be effective. Secrecy can hide the fact that the objectives influencing a decision may represent the personal interests of officials or a small group or class in the community.[21] Secrecy can also keep from view the fact that a very limited number of alternative courses of action were considered, that the thinking about the problem was bounded by ideology or the limited imaginations of the few participants. Anyone who has taken part in decision-making under conditions of secrecy will appreciate how ignorance, lack of imagination, or wilful blindness can damage the effectiveness of government.

Finally, openness is cherished not only for its contributions to democratic effective government but also because it is a central value for a number of professions commonly found in the public service. The codes of conduct of lawyers, doctors, social workers, and health science administrators, for example, place great emphasis on the notion of a free flow of information between professional and client. As Michael Bayles notes: "The responsibility of candor is at the heart of the professional-client relationship."[22] There are relatively few instances, Bayles argues, in which a professional would be justified in withholding information or manipulating information and, thereby, interfering with the client's capacity to make informed judgments and properly consent to a proposed government action.

In the context of the values of participation, accountability, effectiveness, and candour, a strong combination of rights-based and utilitarian arguments can be made in favour of tipping the balance between confidentiality and disclosure in favour of the latter. Mindful of such arguments and the obviously heavy-handed quality of many confidentiality rules, public servants struggle with disclosure dilemmas. If information is power, then public servants are regularly deciding who will have it and who won't. As case 4.1 illustrates, these are often difficult decisions.

**CASE 4.1
ONE DRAFT TOO MANY?**

The following conversation takes place between two middle managers employed in a federal department.

Marion: I've read that policy proposal your team came up with on native housing.

Steve: What did you think of it?

Marion: I thought it was very well done.

Steve: Good, I'm glad. We've been working closely with the Native Council Committee on it. I think it's going to make everyone concerned happy. Now that we've got the final draft prepared, we're going to have a meeting with the committee. We want them to look it over and give us their comments before we send it to the Minister.

Marion: Wait a minute. You can't show them this. That policy proposal is intended for the Minister. That makes it confidential information.

Steve: But I was instructed by the Minister to work closely with the Native Council Committee to devise this policy proposal. My team has worked with Committee members to build the data base for earlier drafts. They are the ones who will be directly affected by this policy if it goes ahead. How can I keep their confidence and trust if I can't show them this draft?

ISSUES

– Could you justify Steve's intention to show the latest draft of the policy proposal to the Native Council Committee?

– Could you construct an argument in favour of keeping the information secret?

Deception, Disinformation, Propaganda, and Censorship

The reference to information manipulation in the context of a professional's duty of candour to a client raises a wider issue. The clash between the duty of confidentiality and the duty of disclosure extends not only to the more obvious question of whether or not to provide certain government information to individual citizens or groups, but also to the acceptability of the practices of deception, disinformation, propaganda, and censorship. The ethical dilemmas associated with such practices are often overlooked because they are traditionally directed towards "enemy" nations or criminals. But it is a mistake to write such activities off as ethically benign. In almost all instances they raise the same concerns as the more common forms of information concealment.

Deception is most commonly practised by governments in undercover police operations. Skeins of often elaborate misinformation are provided to the unwary members of the public to tempt them to act in a criminal manner. The debate about the line between the encouragement of the criminal and the entrapment of the innocent is in large part a debate about the legitimate use of false information.

The sense of unease which may develop when considering the rights and consequences implications of using deception to fight crime often evaporates when the practice of disinformation is considered. Sissela Bok refers to disinformation as "a neologism that stands for the spreading of false information to hurt adversaries. Common in wartime, and increasingly used by contending secret service networks even in peacetime, it now flourishes in the media, as governments try to influence public opinion against one another and against domestic adversaries."[23] But employing disinformation against enemies of the state in wartime when the survival of the society may be at stake is a different proposition from using it for political gain in domestic circumstances. Here public servants can become caught up in the planting of distortions and outright lies in the media. Such practices are usually part of a larger game in which groups opposing the government's position are portrayed as "enemies" and the use of a wide variety of techniques to "defeat" them are rationalized. Consider, for example, the extensive campaign waged by the federal government against the "yes" forces in the sovereignty-association referendum in Quebec in 1980. Federal public servants were heavily involved in what became a no-holds-barred political brawl.

In such circumstances, "pumping up" the government's position and distorting the likely effects of following the opposition's policy may seem relatively harmless activities. But disinformation often goes further to include the spreading of gossip and falsehoods about the leaders of opposition parties or groups as means of discrediting them in the public eye. However far it goes, public servants have to consider carefully the rights of the individuals affected and the corrosive effects of the practice of disinformation on the level of public trust in government and the media.

Parallel arguments can be made about propaganda and censorship. Again these are practices that in wartime have been justified as reasonable and necessary to demoralize the enemy, buoy up your own citizens, and keep strategic information from falling into the hands of the opposing side. But whether used in wartime or applied domestically (outside the context of concerns about the survival of the nation), such practices are merely variations on previously explored themes of secrecy, deception, and disinformation. As such, they raise the full panoply of rights and consequences arguments associated with the tension between disclosure and confidentiality. In addition, censorship directed not at information of strategic significance but rather at material thought to be seditious or immoral raises significant rights issues associated with freedom of expression.

Can Whistle-Blowing be Justified?

While general arguments for or against secrecy in government may help to orient the public servant's overall approach to the handling of confidential information, they do not specifically address the dilemmas confronting the potential whistle-blower. Under what conditions would it be morally permissible or even required to betray one's employer?

First, what kind of actions are encompassed within the term whistle-blowing? We define whistle-blowing broadly as encompassing both the open disclosure or surreptitious leaking to persons outside the organization of confidential information concerning a harmful act that a colleague or superior has committed, is contemplating, or is allowing to occur. We do not treat leaking as a phenomenon separate from whistle-blowing; they both involve the unauthorized release of confidential information, although the choice of method may itself raise ethical dilemmas. We are concerned specifically with the justification of public whistle-blowing. Obviously it is also possible to blow the whistle within the organization, but that does not usually involve making confidential information available to unauthorized recipients. We do, however, take a narrow view of the term organization. While elected representatives or the legislative auditors may be part of the wider government organization, release of confidential information to individuals beyond the boundaries of one's own agency or department is usually described as whistle-blowing even if the recipient (e.g., the auditor general) has a legal right to see such information.

Key characteristics of whistle-blowing are dissent, breach of loyalty, and accusation.[24] The unauthorized release of information is one of the ways in which a public servant can express resistance to the actions (or proposed actions) of government. Dennis Thompson refers to a continuum of dissent or civil disobedience options open to public officials. The continuum includes:

- internal protest combined with continuing co-operation with the development or implementation of the offending policy;

- outside protest (usually in the form of a group statement or petition) in the context of continuing performance of assigned tasks;

- open obstruction of policy, but still within the confines of the organization; and

- covert obstruction, usually through the leaking of classified documents.[25]

The unauthorized disclosure of information is a feature of both outside protest and covert obstruction.

All forms of dissent – and certainly those which involve whistle-blowing – raise the issue of loyalty. As we pointed out in the previous chapter, the meaning and extent of the loyalty of the public servant to his or her superior, agency, and the government in power is a contentious issue. Whistle-blowing tests the boundaries of that loyalty severely by raising the spectre of powerful competing loyalties to the constitution, the law, or even the public servant's perception of the public interest. Peter French argues that "the loyalty claim that stands in conflict with loyalty to a higher ideal (in this case perhaps that is government by the people or merely honest government) is morally illegitimate."[26] He urges public servants to downgrade loyalty in their hierarchy of values, so that loyalty to superiors and the government does not loom in their minds as the ultimate test of the appropriateness of an action.

Finally, whistle-blowing involves the accusation that certain individuals or a group are responsible for the misdeeds in question. As Bok points out, whistle-blowing singles out "those who knew or should have known what was wrong and what the dangers were, and who had the capacity to make different choices."[27]

While the essence of whistle-blowing is the unauthorized release of confidential information, it is the elements of dissent, loyalty, and accusation in this action which make opting to blow the whistle a complex and extremely difficult matter. The presence of these features also accounts for the harsh way in which the publicly exposed whistle-blower is generally treated. He or she is often shunned by colleagues as a "squealer." There is plenty of evidence of attempts at organizational vengeance against the whistle-blower, and even if the culprit moves on to another organization, he or she can be dogged by a reputation for disloyalty and untrustworthiness.[28] These features are not generally considered to be relevant to the moral calculus surrounding whistle-blowing, but they should not be ignored by anybody contemplating such an action. Yet, despite the human costs which the whistle-blower may have to bear, the unauthorized release of confidential information has become a significant phenomenon of modern government. Under what conditions, then, is it morally permissible or even mandatory for a public servant to blow the whistle?[29]

Obviously, such an action would be ethically problematic if the release of information were motivated predominantly by a desire to avenge some action, to improve the whistle-blower's position in the organization (usually at the expense of someone else), or to build support for a desired action when legitimate efforts to gain its acceptance have failed.

One of the key conditions which must be met to make whistle-blowing a morally justifiable option is that the action or omission in question be a seriously harmful one. The whistle-blower must be confident that the transgression has caused or will cause in the near future demonstrably harmful effects. A wide variety of transgressions can qualify under this simple utilitarian test, including instances in which a public official is clearly exceeding the bounds of the constitution, a law, policy, or regulation. Such actions may involve misuse of financial resources, graft, or corruption. The whistle-blower may also be pushed to disclose confidential information in situations in which clear and serious dangers to the public exist – usually in the form of imminent or existing threats to public health or safety – even where a law or regulation is not being violated. More problematic but possibly still compelling grounds for whistle-blowing include cases in which a professional standard is being violated. For example, a government forester may be inclined to blow the whistle on the tree-cutting practices of a company which is operating within government-endorsed regulatory standards but violating standards laid down by the forester's professional association. Even more problematic is a decision to release confidential information about a politically controversial issue where there is room for considerable personal judgment. During the 1930s a senior British public servant revealed defence secrets to Winston Churchill (who was not a member of the cabinet) because he believed strongly that the government was not preparing the nation adequately to meet the military threat from Nazi Germany.[30] The appropriateness of these leaks is still hotly debated by students of British government.

The second test for whistle-blowing is that the accusation of serious harm must be supported by unequivocal evidence. The whistle-blower must be certain that it is possible to demonstrate to the satisfaction of a disinterested observer that his or her assessment of the situation is accurate. Here the whistle-blower has to be satisfied that he or she is taking a wide enough view of the situation and that the possible benefits of a questionable government action are not being ignored due to the whistle-blower's narrow focus on some particular costs. This evidence requirement would tend to reduce the legitimacy of unauthorized disclosure in cases where narrow professional standards or unsupportable judgments of risk to the public were being used as the basis for an accusation. It should also make the whistle-blower conscious of the fact that an accusation which is unsupported by appropriate evidence may be unfair and damaging to the individuals implicated.

To satisfy the third test, the public servant is obliged to ascertain through regularly established channels within the organization that the perceived harm will not be corrected. J. Vernon Jensen puts the key questions very simply:

> Has the whistleblower gone to the immediate supervisor and to other appropriate personnel up the ladder? Has there been an adequate attempt to reason with the wrong-doer(s)? Has the wrong-doer(s) been given enough time to improve the situation? Has the whistleblower demonstrated a positive non-threatening attitude, that is, a genuine desire to correct the problem from within, thus demonstrating one's basic loyalty to the group? In short, has the whistle-

blower sought to keep the problem "in the family" as long as possible?[31]

This requirement to check with supervisors is not always straight-forward. How far up through the organization should a middle- or junior-level public servant be expected to go? While senior officials will often argue that it is unacceptable to go outside a department until the issue has been raised with the deputy minister and even the minister, for junior public servants in a large ministry such a condition may be excessive and unrealistic.[32]

Finally, the potential whistle-blower must have good reasons to expect that the unauthorized disclosure of confidential information will lead to appropriate changes. This "effectiveness" test is self-explanatory, but it also raises a number of important subordinate considerations about how and to whom a public servant should disclose confidential information. Will the credibility of the disclosure be damaged if it is leaked rather than openly brought forward by the whistle-blower? Jensen argues that:

> Keeping one's identity secret obviously carries with it more protection, at least initially, and may embolden the whistle-blower to be more comprehensive and incisive, thus getting to the heart of the case more quickly and effectively. But sooner or later the identity may be revealed, and in the meantime, the credibility will be somewhat suspect, since the whistleblower did not dare to become publicly iden-tified.[33]

If the accusation is made openly would it be more effective for the whistle-blower to resign or stay in his or her post? Staying on the job may be inherently more courageous and pure in the minds of some, but it may have a negative impact on the ability of the whistle-blower's unit to function properly.

Similar "consequence" questions can be raised about the target for the whistle-blower's disclosures. Should he or she go to the press, the police, the government auditor, the ombudsman, or an MLA or MP?[34] The effectiveness test demands that one go to the audience that can do the most to eradicate the problem. If theft of the government's resources is the issue, then the criminal code is probably being violated and the obvious duty is to report this suspicion to the police. Many whistle-blowers lean to informing the ombudsman or an elected

---

CASE 4.2
WHAT ELSE CAN I DO BUT BLOW THE WHISTLE?

This conversation takes place between an employee of the provincial Ministry of Natural Resources and a colleague.

Doug: You look upset, Ellen. What's up?

Ellen: I've been ordered to prepare the paperwork to justify allowing the ACME mining company to start open-pit mining in an area where we haven't even had time to do a proper environmental impact study. They gave me some quickie consultant's report showing that the environmental impact will be minimal, but the study isn't worth the paper it's written on, in my view.

Doug: What exactly are you saying?

Ellen: I'm saying that we aren't following the rules here, Doug. Under the existing regulations ACME can't have a permit without a proper environmental impact certificate from this branch. There must be some reason they're pushing this through.

Doug: Have you mentioned this to your director?

Ellen: Yes, I went to see her and told her what had happened.

Doug: What did she say?

Ellen: She said to go ahead and do as I've been told. Then I went over her head to the assistant deputy minister, and he let me know that it would be inadvisable to raise the matter again. When I asked why, he just pointed upstairs.

Doug: Are you going to leave it at that, Ellen?

Ellen: No... I've decided to tell my MLA...

Doug: What! Are you sure that's what you want to do?

Ellen: If it's wrong to go to your MLA about something like this, who can you turn to? Doug, I've tried internal channels, and haven't gotten anywhere. What alternatives do I have now?

ISSUES

– Do you agree with Ellen's thinking in this case?

– Under what conditions would whistle-blowing be acceptable?

– When should one be satisfied that all internal channels have been exhausted?

– Is whistle-blowing to the media as acceptable as whistle-blowing to an elected representative?

– Would resigning or requesting a transfer be more appropriate?

representative, often because they feel better about disclosing confidential information to someone inside the system. In the last chapter we will discuss the usefulness of an "ethics counsellor," who could advise and assist potential whistle-blowers in finding the most effective audience for their disclosures. It goes without saying that a whistle-blower must have solid reasons for going to the media before directing his or her revelations to targets more likely to be able to effect change. But to return to the basic issue: if the whistle-blower sees no likelihood that unauthorized disclosures will improve the situation, then such an action is probably ill-considered regardless of the target audience chosen.

While a few jurisdictions show signs of recognizing that a public servant may have a positive duty to disclose confidential information under certain circumstances, there is certainly no widespread consensus on the conditions under which such disclosure is tolerable or even required. Ultimately, the public servant is on his or her own when faced with the dilemma of whether or not to "empower" the citizen with confidential information or blow the whistle on government misdeeds. The difficulties associated with working out this dilemma are well illustrated by the circumstances facing Ellen in case 4.2.

Privacy: An Overview of the Ethical Issues

A government's emphasis on secrecy and confidentiality is a reflection of its concern about its own privacy. Therefore, we have been focusing to this point on the nature of the public servant's duty to protect the privacy of government and its decision-makers. But public servants also have a widely accepted duty to protect the privacy of individuals (and even corporations and other governments) that interact with the government for which they work. The duty of confidentiality (or, the duty to protect government privacy) and the duty to protect individual privacy are obviously closely linked. In fact, the protection of the privacy of individuals, corporations, and the records of other governments is one of the key justifications for the duty of confidentiality. But the duty to protect privacy clearly raises ethical questions that range well beyond the issue of how much of the personal information held by governments should be publicly disclosed. These questions include the following:

- What kind of information is it appropriate for a government to be collecting about its citizens?
- How should it be allowed to collect such information (i.e., what forms of surveillance and coercive acquisition are appropriate)?
- What limitations should be placed on the way it manipulates this information?

While the citizen's claim to privacy might appear to be a motherhood issue, troubling questions have emerged about what the duty to protect privacy should mean in the late twentieth century.

What explicit guidance concerning the nature of the duty to protect individual privacy do public servants receive from the web of rules and conventions within which they operate? The short answer is that it depends upon the government for which you work. It is unusual to find specific references to the protection of privacy in oaths of office or codes of conduct for public servants anywhere in Canada. Article 5 of the Quebec Charter of Human Rights and Freedoms maintains that "every person has a right to respect for his private life," but not even this tentative protection is available in the Canadian Charter of Rights and Freedoms which is completely silent on the issue of privacy.[35] Three provinces have privacy acts which make it a civil offense to violate the privacy of an individual, but they are so limited in scope that they provide no useful direction to the public servant about the abuse of personal information. Despite its name, the federal Protection of Privacy Act of 1974 actually legalizes wiretapping in the course of criminal investigations.

Only Quebec, Ontario, and the federal government have privacy legislation which speaks directly to the abuse of personal privacy by public officials. These pieces of legislation regulate the collection, retention, disposal, correction, and dissemination of personal information by government and establish principles of fair information practice. These principles include the following:

- The individual has a right to know why the information is being collected.
- Collect only sufficient information needed to do the job at hand.
- Use information only for the purpose for which it was collected.

- No secret data banks are permissible.
- Individuals have a right of access to their own information.
- Individuals have the right to annotate or correct information on themselves which they believe to be faulty, incomplete, or irrelevant.

Unfortunately, these rules are far from universal and, as the annual reports of the existing privacy protection agencies make clear, are regularly violated even in the jurisdictions where they hold sway. Violations attributable to carelessness and technical error are regrettable, but of little ethical significance. What does interest us is the degree to which the duty of privacy and the principles of fair information practice are overridden in the minds of public servants by other duties and values. Public servants do not appear to attach a particularly high level of priority to the protection of individual privacy. There are instances of officials becoming willing participants in schemes to identify publicly individuals who provided data anonymously, supplying sensitive government data to commercial users, turning information over to politicians, police, and intelligence operations without permission, combining data sets without authorization, and collecting "extra" data from recipients of state services. The type of dilemma confronted by Frankie in case 4.3 is becoming all too common.

In part, the duty to protect privacy may be given short shrift by public servants because they are reflecting a wider societal uncertainty about the value of privacy. This uncertainty is rooted in confusion about what privacy means. Arthur Schafer summarizes the problem of meaning in the following way:

> It is surprisingly difficult to give a straightforward definition of the concept of privacy. Despite innumerable attempts by contemporary philosophers and jurists to formulate a definition, the concept has remained elusive. One can discover no consensus in either the legal or philosophical literature.[36]

The traditional approach to privacy equates it with non-interference, the right to be left alone to live one's life with the minimum of interference. Schafer argues that a non-interference approach to defining privacy is necessary because it covers situations where others are intrusively observing us (e.g., surveillance). But it is

---

CASE 4.3
THE MINISTER WANTS TO KNOW

This conversation takes place between two provincial Ministry of Human Resources employees.

Cary: I want you to conduct an internal information search on three of our clients.

Frankie: What for? Are we checking for welfare fraud?

Cary: No. The minister's office has requested the information.

Frankie: What's this all about?

Cary: Apparently, these three people were involved in a demonstration for welfare rights last week. They've been harassing the minister about the new regulations announced last week on income assistance.

Frankie: Wait a minute... Internal information searches are usually reserved for child abuse or welfare fraud investigations. I can't just send out a memo requesting information on people because their organization has been pestering the minister. That's an invasion of privacy!

Cary: Look, I know it's a bit unusual, but the minister has specifically asked me to try to find out something about them. I can't just go back there empty-handed. Besides, if these people have been harassing the minister, we owe him this much.

ISSUES

- Is Cary's request reasonable?
- Should Frankie do as he is told? Or does he have a greater duty to protect the privacy of income assistance clients?
- Does "harassment" of the minister justify an investigation of this type?
- If not, can you think of a situation in which such an investigation might be warranted?

---

inadequate for many critics because privacy is easily invaded without any interference (e.g., your photograph is taken from a distance) and interference can occur without any diminution of privacy (e.g., limitations on freedom of expression). Moreover, it is insufficient because it doesn't deal easily with situations in which loss of control over personal information is the crux of the issue. To deal with the latter phenomenon, Alan Westin defines privacy as "the claim of individuals, groups or institutions to determine for themselves when, how, and to what extent information about them is communicated to others."37   Together, "non-interference" and "information control" approaches to defining privacy seem to capture a considerable portion of what we mean by the term, but only at the expense of remaining vague and ambiguous.   When there is so little clarity about what is being protected, is it surprising that it is so readily violated?

It should not have escaped notice that Alan Westin refers to privacy as a claim, not a right.   The implication is that privacy is an important but far from absolute value.   Within our liberal democratic state, individual privacy is seen as an essential ingredient in the exercise of free political choice, the maintenance of family life, and the enhancement of individual creativity.   On a more personal level, privacy is necessary to maintain individual autonomy, to allow for emotional release, to carry on self-evaluation and to protect intimate personal communications.38   These functions of privacy form the basis of a powerful consequential argument in its favour.   Privacy promotes the individual and social relationships of love, trust, and respect which are essential to our integrity as persons.   Deontological defences of privacy complement the utilitarian claims.39

> Even when no extrinsic harm comes to a person as a result of losing his or her privacy, that person has a *prima facie* ground for claiming the right not to be spied upon or watched without knowledge or consent.   Humans are self-conscious beings.   To monitor their conduct without authorization is to show a less-than-proper respect for their dignity.40

But there are also strong arguments against attaching too much importance to privacy.   Schafer observes that "[a] number of Western social scientists have argued that privacy has become an unhealthy obsession of contemporary liberal society."41   It breeds alienation, discontent, family-based solitude, and an egoistic man, engrossed in competitiveness and self-fulfilment and indifferent to his fellow man and the wider community.

It is ideas such as these that underlie the willingness of social scientists and public servants to sacrifice privacy in favour of other values.   It has been argued that privacy should give way to openness more frequently when choices are being made about the release of

---

CASE 4.4
LET'S ROOT OUT THE CHEATERS

The following conversation takes place between Diane, a director, and Stuart, an assistant director in the Provincial Treasury Board Secretariat.

Diane: The problem of welfare fraud is a serious one, Stuart. Have you come up with any suggestions on how to tackle it?

Stuart: Yes, I think so. I propose a merger of several administrative data sets related to income maintenance programs. We could link them to government personnel records, vehicle ownership data, and the files of the marriage, birth, personal assets, and land registries. If we could gain access to them, we could even bring in personal financial records.

Diane: We've got to be careful here. You can't go using that information for reasons other than the ones it was collected for. This proposal involves violating the individual's right to privacy.

Stuart: Diane, you told me yourself that welfare fraud is getting out of hand. We've got to do something to control it. If the program clients have told their case officers the truth, there won't be any problem. If they lied, don't we have a right to know?

Diane: I'm not so sure . . .

Stuart: I've already spoken to your boss about this, Diane. He thinks it's a good idea.

ISSUES

– Would you subscribe to an action of this sort to cut down on welfare fraud? Why? Why not?

– In a welfare state should individuals expect to have their right to privacy restricted to some degree?

– Is informed consent an issue here?

– Is data-matching of this type any different from having a social worker drop in "unexpectedly" for a visit?

– Was it appropriate for Stuart to go over Diane's head with his plan?

confidential information containing data on identifiable individuals or corporations. Journalists and researchers are often blocked from access to records which reveal the actions or advice of individual public officials or citizens.[42] The Ontario Commission on Freedom of Information and Individual Privacy concluded that "the rationale of open government provides a competing interest which, in appropriate cases, will have a higher claim."[43] Public servants are also attracted by arguments which suggest that government can be made cheaper, more efficient, and effective and even fairer if more data are collected on citizens and modern computer technology is used to integrate and manipulate these data. Why, they ask, when citizens and corporations are the beneficiaries of so many government services and subsidiaries, is it legitimate for them to make such extensive privacy claims? As case 4.4 suggests, why can't we go further in matching information from unemployment insurance claims, income tax and welfare payments to prevent the state paying double benefits? Why not use computer linkage to find those who fail to support their children? Furthermore, questions have been raised about the appropriate balance between the privacy of the individual and the health or security of the wider population. When should compulsory AIDS tests be permitted? Why cannot AIDS-related personal information be released? Why not insist on compulsory drug-testing or psychological profiles for public transport employees? Should governments be given the power to test citizens surreptitiously for substance abuse or infectious diseases? In short, what is the nature of the "new" balance that needs to be struck between individual and corporate privacy on the one hand, and efficient, effective, fair, and open administration on the other?

Conclusion

In this chapter we have discussed how a public servant should deal with information. How much openness is enough? There is obviously a balance to be struck between a completely transparent process and the ability to function effectively. It is possible that openness may be a good policy to stop bad things from happening, but may be ill-conceived as a means to get good things to occur.[44] The trick is to find the middle ground between the paralysis of government in a gold-fish bowl and the over-concentration of power inherent in an information monopoly.

Even if that balance point or middle ground can be found, it won't necessarily be helpful in dealing with a potential whistle-blowing case where dissent and betrayal are central features of the dilemma.

How much privacy is enough? There is a parallel balance to be struck between the claim to non-interference and information control on the one side, and the information needs of complex program structures driven by concerns about abuse, efficiency, and effectiveness on the other. Searching for such balance points is the essence of responsible public service.

Notes

1. Ontario Law Reform Commission (OLRC), *Report on Political Activity, Public Comment and Disclosure by Crown Employees,* (Toronto: Ministry of the Attorney General, 1986), pp. 33-73.

2. The most notable exceptions are the governments of Nova Scotia and Quebec. The latter lays down a duty of confidentiality in its Public Service Act, 6; the former depends on the wider common law obligation of confidentiality.

3. See OLRC, *Report,* p. 161.

4. Ibid., p. 100, 101-102.

5. Office of the Prime Minister, release, November 23, 1984. These guidelines appear to have been taken almost verbatim from a directive issued to public servants by the Ontario government in October 1980.

6. Freedom of Information and Personal Privacy Act, s. 74.

7. Government of British Columbia, "Personnel Management Policies and Procedures," General Policies chapter, Standards of Conduct section.

8. The exception at the provincial level is Nova Scotia, which provides access only to defined categories of information. See OLRC *Report,* p. 164.

9. See OLRC, *Report,* pp. 51-74.

10. See *Open and Shut: Enhancing the Right to Know and the Right to Privacy,* Report of the Standing Committee on Justice and Solicitor General on the Review of the Access to Information Act

and the Privacy Act (Ottawa: Supply and Services Canada, 1987), p. 86.

11. Quoted in ibid.

12. Law Reform Commission of Canada, *Crimes Against the State*, Working Paper 49 (Ottawa: Supply and Services Canada, 1986), Chs. 3 and 4: and OLRC, *Report*, pp. 101-103.

13. Sissela Bok, *Secrets: On the Ethics of Concealment and Revelation* (New York: Random House, 1983), p. 172.

14. Gordon Robertson, "Official Responsibility, Private Conscience and Public Information," *Optimum* 3, no. 3 (1972), p. 12.

15. Bok, *Secrets*, p. 192.

16. Donald Smiley, *The Freedom of Information Issue: A Political Analysis* (Toronto: Commission on Freedom of Information and Individual Privacy, 1978), p. 23.

17. See *Public Government for Private People: The Report of the Commission on Freedom of Information and Individual Privacy* (Toronto: Queen's Printer, 1980), vol. 2, ch. 20; See also, Joseph Margolis, "Democracy and the Responsibility to Inform the Public" in Norman E. Bowie, ed., *Ethical Issues in Government* (Philadelphia: Temple University Press, 1981), ch. 15.

18. *Public Government for Private People* 2:81. This argument is raised again in ch. 5.

19. Harlan Cleveland, "How Much Sunshine Is Too Much," *Across the Board* (July/August 1985), p. 18.

20. David Curzon, "The Generic Secrets of Government Decision Making" in Itzhak Galnoor, ed., *Government Secrecy in Democracies* (New York: NY Press, 1977), ch. 6.

21. Ibid., p. 103.

22. Michael D. Bayles, *Professional Ethics* (Belmont, Mass.: Wadsworth Publishing Company, 1981), p. 72. Bayles defines candour as a combination of truthfulness and full disclosure.

23. Bok, *Secrets*, p. 187.

24. Ibid., p. 214.

25. Dennis F. Thompson, "The Possibility of Administrative Ethics," *Public Administration Review* 45 (September/October 1985), pp. 557-58.

26. Peter A. French, *Ethics in Government* (Englewood Cliffs, N.J.: Prentice Hall, 1983), p. 136.

27. Bok, *Secrets*, p. 215.

28. See Marcia A. Parmerlee et al., "Correlates of Whistle-Blowers' Perception of Organizational Retaliation," *Administrative Science Quarterly* 27 (March 1982), pp. 17-34.

29. See the set of questions raised in Kenneth Kernaghan, "The Conscience of the Bureaucrat: Accomplice or Constraint?", *Canadian Public Administration* 27 (Winter 1984), p. 590.

30. See Martin Gilbert, *Winston S. Churchill*, Vol. 5: *1922-39* (London: Heinemann, 1976), p. 555.

31. J. Vernon Jensen, "Ethical Tension Points in Whistleblowing," *Journal of Business Ethics* 6, no. 4 (May 1987), p. 322.

32. The British Columbia Standards of Conduct specify that a public servant bring an "issue to the attention of the Deputy Minister, either directly or through normal ministry channels" before going outside the ministry.

33. Jensen, "Ethical Tension Points," p. 323. Anonymous leaking may also allow the public servant to keep on top of the resolution of the problem and confirm the effectiveness of the solutions proposed.

34. The B.C. Standards of Conduct spell out that "an allegation of illegal activities should be referred to the Auditor General; a danger to public health should be brought to the attention of the health authorities (e.g., Public Health Inspectors); and any safety concerns should be dealt with by established procedures (e.g., Safety Committees)."

35. This section draws on the review of the legal framework for the protection of individual privacy contained in David H. Flaherty, "After 1984: The Protection of Privacy in Canada," a paper prepared for delivery to the annual conference of Canadian Legislative Ombudsmen, Vancouver, B.C., September 13, 1983.

36. Arthur Schafer, "Privacy: A Philosophical Overview," in Dale Gibson, ed., *Aspects of Privacy Law* (Toronto: Butterworths,

1980), p. 4. This discussion of the meaning of privacy draws on Schafer's analysis.

37. Alan Westin, *Privacy and Freedom* (New York: Atheneum, 1967), p. 7.

38. Ibid., ch. 2.

39. Shafer, "Privacy," p. 16.   See also S.I. Benn, "Privacy, Freedom and Respect for Persons," in J.R. Pennock and J.W. Chapman, eds., *Nomos 13:   Privacy* (New York: Atherton Press, 1971), pp. 1-3.

40. Shafer, "Privacy," p. 17.

41. Ibid., p. 18.

42. See John D. McCamus, "The Delicate Balance: Reconciling Privacy Protection with the Freedom of Information Principle," and T. Murray Rankin, "Access to Information and Barriers for Privacy: The Search for Balance," both papers presented to the Conference on Privacy Initiatives for 1984, Toronto.

43. *Public Government for Private People*, p. 324.

44. See Cleveland's provocative ideas around this theme in Harlan Cleveland, "The Twilight of Hierarchy: Speculations on the Global Information Society," *Public Administration Review* 45 (January/February 1985), pp. 190-91.

Chapter 5

Service to the Public

If public service is not about service to the public, then what is it about? This duty of service to the public, implicit and largely unspoken or ignored for so long, has emerged in recent years as a central preoccupation of the shapers of public sector management values. In part this development may have been inspired by the increased private sector emphasis on the "customer." But even without a push from the world of commerce, the massive growth of government activities and bureaucratic discretion over the last three decades would, inevitably, have provoked a backlash of concern about the degree to which the fundamental value of "service" had been allowed to languish.

In this chapter we will try to "unpack" the duty of service to the public, and examine what obligations it places upon the public servant. What we will find is that there is widespread agreement about the importance of this duty; few public servants would deny that the "purpose of any governmental activity or program is to provide service to a clientele, a public."[1] This consensus has contributed to the fragmented state of the efforts to justify the duty of service to the public: why spend time defending what seems so obvious? It has also

111

masked the fact that there is little agreement among public servants, politicians, and academic experts about how key components of this duty should be defined and the relative significance of these components. In effect, we are dealing here with a duty, the internal components of which may often be both misunderstood and at war with each other.

Defining the Duty

When the the subject of service to the public is brought up in ordinary conversation, most people think of a face-to-face or telephone transaction with a public servant. When they arrive at the counter as a customer they want efficiency. In other words, they expect the wicket to be open at convenient times and they expect prompt and competent attention to their concerns. They also want to be treated courteously. Moreover, they want the service to meet their needs – to be effective. Finally, they want the reassurance that they are being treated fairly, that is, receiving the same treatment as others unless relevant reasons to treat them differently have been presented. In short, in all of their dealings with the public, public servants are expected to be courteous, efficient, effective, and fair.[2]

That public servants recognize the legitimacy of a duty of service to the public does not seem to be in doubt. Such an obligation is reflected in the codes of conduct of a number of the professional groups which make up the public service. The Institute of Public Administration of Canada, for instance, enshrines the notion in its Statement of Principles. "Public employees," it states, "should provide service to the public in a manner which is courteous, equitable, efficient and effective." In fact, it goes further and enjoins public servants to "be sensitive and responsive to the changing needs, wishes and rights of the public" and "to promote excellence in public service." Finally, it insists on the public servants' duty "to treat members of the public and one another fairly and to ensure that their work environment is free from discrimination and harassment."[3]

Values such as competence, courtesy, efficiency, effectiveness, fairness, and accessibility are found in a variety of guises in the codes of conduct of professionals working in government. In addition, many of these codes focus particular attention on the allocation of responsibility in decision-making between the professional and the

client. On this subject, there is less constancy in the signal provided to
the affected public servants. Some codes (e.g., for lawyers) tend to see
the professional being directed by the client. Others (e.g., for
accountants, engineers, health care professionals) portray the client
and professional as full partners in decision-making or place the
professional in a paternalistic relationship with the client, with the
latter being incapable of meaningful participation in complex
technical and value decisions. The fiduciary model alleviates the
latter problem by portraying the professional as the provider of
technical information, alternatives, and analysis of costs and benefits,
but leaving key decisions to the client.[4] Despite such differences, the
general message to professionals is that service to the public – as
client – is the essence of their role.

Governments themselves have also begun to stress the duty of
service to the public. The federal government's Task Force on Service
to the Public established ten principles: service delivery should be
consumer-oriented, timely, sensitive to the public's needs, and
equitable; it should also be accompanied by appropriate levels of
information and be provided with due regard for the rights of
individuals, their comfort, convenience, safety, and security; and
finally, the public must be provided with recourse and response in the
event of dissatisfaction.[5] This set of rules was repeated almost
verbatim in the Treasury Board's Principles for the Management of
the Public Service,[6] where the obligation to provide the public with
channels of communication for participation in program development
and assessment was added to the set of duties. Both statements also
stress the public servant's duty to optimize program economy,
efficiency, and effectiveness; or, put another way, to optimize the
"responsible" use of available resources.

These themes were revived within the federal government by the
1987 report of the Committee on Governing Values. This committee,
composed of deputy ministers, portrayed government as primarily a
service enterprise. In searching for an overriding value it put this
question: "Could we say that we exist only to serve; to serve the people
of Canada, wherever they are located, either directly and/or indirectly;
to serve the Ministers, the Government and Parliament and in serving
them, to again serve the people of Canada?" They asked if such a
service philosophy could be transformed into "a statement which we
would be proud to advertise, one which summarizes what we are about
and what we believe in. Would it look like this:

PEOPLE SERVING PEOPLE

OUR mission is SERVICE
Our PRODUCT is SERVICE
Our goal is superior SERVICE

We believe that service must be based on:

RESPECT
RESPONSIBILITY and
RESPONSIVENESS.

As public servants we want to:

- put people before things
- put our clients before ourselves
- aim for excellence in everything we do
- create a growing, learning environment
- be creative and innovative
- have strong leadership, and
- work as a team.

*When we do these things our clients will know that
we are:*

- serving them to
- serve our country, and
- are a unique and special service."[7]

The re-emergence of service to the public as a major duty is not limited to the federal government. The Statement of Organizational Philosophy of the District of West Vancouver states that: "This organization exists for the purpose of maintaining and enhancing the quality of the physical, social and economic environments valued by our community for the benefit of the citizens through effective service by all our employees."[8]

A 1986 values clarification exercise by the Ontario public service established "excellence in service to the public" as the highest objective.[9] Within service to the public are included prompt, courteous, helpful responses to public requests for assistance or information, and the principle that actions of public servants be consistent. The Alberta public service code of conduct begins with the statement: "The people of Alberta have a right to public service which is conducted with efficiency, impartiality and integrity."[10] The City of Ottawa has recently begun to focus employee and public attention on "the achievement of excellence in local government," through service improvement defined as "making good things better by improving our service to you, while keeping costs down . . . You, our client, will also be asked to participate in Service Improvement by identifying those things which are important to you, such as cost and level of services, quality, cleanliness, courtesy and security."[11]

This re-emphasis on the duty of service to the public is not confined to Canada. For example, the government of Ireland brought out a white paper in 1985 entitled "Serving the Country Better" which dealt in some detail with the importance of "meeting the citizen's needs." The Organization for Economic Cooperation and Development (OECD) climbed on the band wagon with its report entitled *Administration as Service*, in which it provided an overview of the renewed emphasis which all member governments (including Canada) are placing on "responsive administration." A service-oriented administration, according to the OECD, should be comprehensible and accessible, "engage the participation of clients in the administrative process," and "satisfy client needs effectively and fairly within the limits and objectives set by government policy."[12]

While there is obviously room for considerable debate about the exact definition of the duty of service to the public (especially where a professional is involved in a direct relationship with a client), there is no doubt that some variation on this theme is held out by most governments and professional groups involved in government as an essential obligation of all public servants.

We are at the moment in the midst of a veritable upsurge of interest in the spirit of public service among public sector managers. A commitment to service is identified as a critical attribute of both the "well-performing" government organization[13] and the "new managerialism" emerging in the public sector.[14] Unlike the duty to act in the public interest, where public servants are given virtually no sense of direction about how to go about it, this duty can be (and is) given operational meaning usually in terms of key values which, if adhered to by public servants and their organizations, will result in good service to the public.[15] By contrast with the duty of confidentiality, where public servants may be faced with diametrically opposed sets of instructions concerning the dissemination of confidential information, the duty of service to the public seems, on the surface, relatively straightforward.

Justifying the Duty of Service to the Public

At the most universal level, a duty of service to the public flows from the fundamental role of public bureaucracies in a liberal democratic society. Public servants in a modern democracy are provided with enormous discretionary power in the management of society's resources and the handling of significant aspects of citizens' lives. A fundamental obligation within the democratic system is that this discretionary power not be abused. Efficiency, effectiveness, consistency, competence, fairness, responsiveness, and accessibility have long been recognized as key administrative values which flow from a society's commitment to the liberal democratic model.[16] Public servants have a duty not only to identify the widest public interest in the exercise of discretionary power, but also to exercise that power in a manner which reflects their responsibility to the affected individuals as citizens and fellow human beings.[17]

A parallel form of justification is generally employed to legitimize more specific norms for professional-client relationships. Bayles argues that "norms for professional roles are to be justified by their promoting and preserving the values of liberal society." He takes a fundamentally deontological approach to resolving conflicts between the values or rights of professionals, clients, and the wider public. Balance between these rights "is determined by considering what a reasonable person holding liberal values would desire for himself or herself in the respective roles."[18]

But there are problems associated with using the liberal democratic model alone as a rationale for a broadly based duty of service to the public. As we shall point out in chapter 7, our particular variation on the model, the system of responsible cabinet government, places considerable emphasis on the "objective" responsibility of public servants to their superiors and political masters and much less on their "subjective" responsibility to the public and colleagues. This has the effect of placing a sense of duty of service to the public lower down in the hierarchy of obligations than advocates of the importance of this duty might accept.

But this hierarchy of responsibilities argument is not a problem for the school of thought which insists that "a special relationship should exist between public servants and citizens" in a democracy. Frederickson and Hart, for instance, argue that "along with the commitment to correct principles, public servants must genuinely care for their fellow citizens." The justification for this special relationship "lies in a conception of political community which is defined by the existence of a pervasive patriotism based upon benevolence." They define the primary moral obligation of public servants as "an extensive love of all people" within the political boundaries of the country and "the imperative that they must be protected in all of the basic rights granted to them by the enabling documents".[19] The federal Committee on Governing Values was making a similar point when it asked whether the nature of public service in the context of the constitution and the Charter of Rights and Freedoms did not demand special obligations of public servants including:

- putting the rights and needs of the nation and our clients before our personal interest;
- recognizing that Canadians have a right to equitable treatment in their dealing with government and in their participation in government; . . .
- being sensitive and responsive to the rights and changing needs of our clients.[20]

This line of argument is supported by Peter French, who contends that, in addition to competence and efficiency, public servants owe the public kindness, charity, and benevolence. French focuses his attention specifically on the issue of *how* public servants behave toward members of the public rather than *what* they do to them. In other words, he is not suggesting that the obligation to be kind or benevolent precludes the proper administration of just laws which might involve hardships or unpleasantness for the citizen. His point is that:

Although a bureaucrat may be perfectly justified legally and morally in performing some action on a private citizen (indeed, he or she may be required to do it), the manner of the performance may be morally unworthy, a discredit to his or her character. Doing what is morally right is one thing, and its moral importance is not to be diminished, but doing what is right is not always enough. Being in the right ought not to be a club to batter the dignity of another human

being, to make an action justifiably taken against that
person more unbearable than it needs to be.[21]

At root, this position is deontological in character. It extends to the
relationship between the public servant and the public a strong form of
the "golden rule," thereby enhancing the defence of the duty of service
to the public which flows from our model of democratic government.

But the defence of this duty does not end with references to our
underlying political philosophy or the elevation of the virtues of
kindness, charity, and benevolence. A number of the key specific
obligations making up the duty of service to the public find their
justification in strongly rooted middle-level theories. The preoccupation with efficiency can be traced to the theories of scientific
management. "From Weber to Wilson to Goodnow to White to Gulick
and Urwick one finds a rather consistent development of the notion
that the chief task of public administrators is to achieve efficiency in
the implementation of policy through the application of generic
scientific principles."[22] In recent years the concept of effectiveness has
been grafted on to efficiency and economy to make a compelling value
"package" which government auditors have been strongly fostering.

Fairness is another key value within the duty of service to the
public which draws on powerful theories of natural justice or due
process for legitimization. Both the courts and, more recently,
ombudsmen have been strong proponents of the notion that impartial
treatment of members of the public who come into contact with
government is the essence of being a responsible public servant. It is
essential to note, however, that while the duty of procedural fairness is
founded most immediately in legal theory, its roots go back to a more
basic deontological principle. Peter Wilenski points out that even
Black's law dictionary insists that the spirit and habit of fairness,
justice, and right dealing is merely an extension of the golden rule.[23]
In this sense, the obligation to treat other people impartially is a
fundamental moral duty dictated by the rational principle of reciprocity: if you don't respect other people's interests, you can hardly expect
them to respect yours.

Another basic principle used to justify the duty of fairness is the
right of individuals to consent to actions that affect their interests.
But the defence of fairness need not be exclusively deontological in
character. As we shall see, strong utilitarian arguments can be made
to justify grafting an obligation to consult with the public onto the

notion of fairness. Consultation, it is argued by some, makes for more efficient, effective, and conflict-free governance.[24]

More recently, attempts have been made to add values enhancing "excellence" to the package of values making up the duty of service to the public. This effort has been driven by the parallel attempts to redefine the principles that characterize successful business management in the private sector.[25] While a number of critics have attacked the notion that autonomy and entrepreneurship, for instance, are desirable public sector values, some of the principles embraced by the "excellence" movement (most notably, staying close to the customer) seem quite compatible with the aims of a public sector service philosophy.[26]

All of this is not intended to obscure the fact that it is possible to construct a simple utilitarian defence for most actions designed to enhance service to the public. Clients that are treated efficiently, effectively, fairly, and courteously are happier clients. They complain less, thereby increasing the efficiency and morale of the organization and reducing the need for "catch-up" efforts to bring them on side or redress their procedural grievances.

Fuzzy Signals on Efficiency and Effectiveness

The public seems to have a fairly clear idea of what is meant by efficient and effective service. The former is service that is reliably, competently, and quickly delivered; the latter is service that is relevant, helping to solve your problem as opposed to making it worse or missing the point completely. Efficient and effective service is also responsive to the changing needs of the public. Unfortunately, while these two values may appear straightforward to the public, they are often far from clear to public servants, who get conflicting signals from a variety of sources about both the meaning and importance of efficiency and effectiveness.

To the auditors, financial officers, central controllers, and other players in the program evaluation industry which has grown up in and around contemporary government, efficiency and effectiveness are technical values, useful to measure organizational performance and assist in the process of holding public servants accountable for the consequences of their actions. Efficiency, within this context, becomes little more than a measure of labour productivity, while effectiveness is a reflection of the impact of a program on its stated objectives.[27]

Is it surprising that, in an organizational environment preoccupied since the early 1970s by technical approaches to the measurement of performance, the public's perspective on the meaning of efficiency and effectiveness might become lost and the two values reduced to little more than handy internal management tools? Is it surprising, further, that the cost-oriented approach to efficiency and effectiveness is the driving force behind policy decisions which have the effect of standardizing, reducing, and eliminating services to the public? At the onset of the preoccupation with technical approaches to performance measurement, Al Johnson warned of the inherent conflict between the values of "administrative efficiency" (as he labelled the productivity approach) and "service efficiency" (his term for the public's common-sense approach to efficiency).

> I am not suggesting by any means that we should ignore administrative efficiency: quite the contrary, it is one of our primary goals. But I do suggest that as public servants we have a responsibility to look to the broader kinds of efficiency as well – "policy efficiency" and "service efficiency" – if we are to serve the public well.[28]

To follow through on this advice, public servants would have to pay significant attention to subjective measures of performance such as client reaction and satisfaction rather than the more widely endorsed technical measures of efficiency and effectiveness.[29]

The meaning and significance of efficiency and effectiveness are further clouded for public servants by the views of politicians on these issues. For ministers and government backbenchers, fixated by concerns about electoral popularity, neither the perspective of individual members of the public nor the narrow technical vision of the evaluators represent an entirely reasonable approach to efficiency and effectiveness. For politicians, efficient public service is that which generates few complaints; public service is effective when it makes a lot of voters happy, regardless of cost or the relationship of the results achieved to the ostensible purposes of the program. In fact, the appearance of effectiveness might be a lot more important to politicians than the real thing.

While the politicians' approach to efficiency and effectiveness may not be incompatible in all respects with the common-sense perspective of the public, the combination of these disparate signals from politicians and central agencies presents the public servant with a confused message concerning both the meaning and importance which should be attached to the values of efficiency and effectiveness.

Some observers argue that this confusion is further enhanced by the very nature of bureaucratic organization, which is at odds not only with the public's perception of efficiency and effectiveness, but with the whole concept of service to the public. Bureaucracy is ideally adapted to bringing large numbers of people together to work on big tasks. But the necessary fixation of bureaucratic organizations with power, control, maintenance, survival, and standardization makes them, almost by nature, hostile to the values we have identified with the duty of service to the public.[30] Hummel argues that bureaucracy transforms social action into what Weber referred to as "rationally organized action":

> In brief, the way bureaucrats relate to clients is analogous to the way people in one country relate to people from an entirely different country. Bureaucrats can't help the way they act – if they want to remain employed members of bureaucracy. There is something innate in bureaucracy that turns bureaucrats into people who provide service coldly, impersonally, without a frown or a smile.[31]

If they responded to the dominant values of the bureaucratic culture, public servants would become detached from their clients, transforming people into "cases" and focusing only on the "facts" that are "relevant" to the narrow "processing" task that their job description defines for them. The powerful demands of routine, manuals, and rules would tend to distance the bureaucrat from the citizen and force the values we have associated with the duty of service to the public to the back of the bus.[32] Especially when dealing with disadvantaged and powerless clients, it can be a short step from indifference and distance to bullying and hostility.

It is argued further that professionalism is not the antidote to this pervasive bureaucratic culture that it was once thought to be. Drucker and others believed that professionalization of the public service would temper or offset the values which seem antithetical to the duty of service to the public and lead to "the development of more flexible and creative modes of operation."[33] Instead, the evidence from the United States suggests that the public-oriented values of service delivery professionals appear to have been overwhelmed by the dominant bureaucratic culture:

> As a particular public service occupation moves down the path of professionalism, a typical pattern is for it to develop national, uniform standards of behaviour and then, increasingly, to establish bureaucratic controls and processes designed to ensure the application of these standards . . . The accommodation to bureaucracy is taking place at the expense of one of the hallmarks of the true professional: the commitment to service.[34]

CASE 5.1
DOING IT BY THE BOOK

Mark is a purchasing agent and Mary a middle manager in a large government ministry.

Mark: I've been receiving a number of purchase orders from your division, Mary. You've been buying a lot of office equipment lately – one piece at a time.

Mary: I know it looks strange on paper. Look, I'll be straight with you Mark. We're outfitting one of our offices.

Mark: That's what I thought. But why are you sending in your purchase orders one item at a time?

Mary: Originally, I went through the Department of Supply and Services. They told me a complete system would cost $50,000. That's absolutely ridiculous! I know for a fact that if I buy those components separately through a wholesaler I can get the whole system for $40,000.

Mark: You know the rules, Mary. Any purchase order for amounts greater than $3,000 requires Treasury Board approval through the Department of Supply and Services.

Mary: But if I do it by the book it will cost $10,000 more. Why should I waste all that money for no reason?

ISSUES

– Did Mary behave responsibly in breaking the rules to save her division money?

– If so, is it appropriate to ignore any rule which seems to foster waste or inefficiency? Where do you draw the line?

– Should Mark overlook the fact that Mary has deviated from normal procedure in this case?

Government auditors and the media regularly confront the public with incidents in which bureaucratic rules clash with values such as efficiency and effectiveness (as defined by either technocrats or the public). In such a case would it be responsible for a public servant to break or bend the rules in order to reduce public expenditure, increase productivity, or adapt the service being provided more closely to the clients' needs? Are there specific circumstances in which such an action might be justified? In case 5.1 Mark confronts Mary with the fact that she has been breaking the rules.

This ongoing debate about the appropriate meaning and significance to be attached to basic values such as efficiency and effectiveness does not leave the public servant in a very comfortable position. In a sense, it is a question of loyalty: which vision of these key values should prevail when there is potential for conflict? How important is the public servant's duty to serve the public relative to obligations to his or her political masters, organization, or profession? A parallel question of loyalty focusing on the issue of political neutrality was raised in chapter 3, and a further variation on this theme will emerge from the discussion of accountability in chapter 7.

How Much Fairness is Enough?

The debate about the appropriate meaning and limits to be placed on the value of fairness is perhaps even more compelling than the battles over efficiency and effectiveness. Being fair means different things to different people. For some it conjures up notions of administrative impartiality and consistency and roughly translates into the basic rules of procedural fairness that have evolved with administrative law. For others, fairness means going considerably further to "level the playing field" for members of the public who are trying to protect or enhance their interests in the face of government intervention. This latter vision of fairness embraces the notions of participation, consultation, and accessibility. Both approaches to fairness raise hard questions about how much fairness is enough.

Basic procedural fairness is a key element of good service to the public. It has been demonstrated by a number of studies that individuals dealing with government are willing to accept inequality of treatment as long as the process by which inequalities are decided upon are themselves equitable or fair and the grounds upon which discrimination is based are clear and reasonable.[35]   Where public servants are wielding their discretionary power to distribute limited state resources among competing individuals or groups, the concept of procedural fairness places the following obligations on them:

- Don't avoid decisions that you are empowered to make, but do not become involved in decisions beyond your legitimate authority;
- Avoid bias and even the appearance of conflict of interest;
- Provide a hearing to those people whose interests are significantly affected by a decision;
- Allow those who feel they have been dealt with unfairly some form of recourse or appeal.

Gillian Andrews sums up the duty this way:

> The "rules of natural justice" is the name given to the requirement that people whose rights will be affected be given an opportunity to present their case to the decision-maker, and that it is the duty of the decision-maker to listen to both sides, and to make a fair decision which is untainted by bias.[36]

These rules of procedural fairness are upheld by courts and ombudsmen, and would seem to be widely accepted. However, there are some dissenting voices. Professionals, particularly those providing human services, often argue that the duties associated with procedural fairness can make it difficult for them to operate effectively, reducing their flexibility and ability to respond adequately to the specific needs of clients. They argue, in part, that procedural fairness often combines with technical notions of efficiency to produce a sterile standardization of service unrelated to the needs of individual clients.[37]

Those preoccupied by the value of technical efficiency have a parallel gripe of their own: that procedural fairness makes the exercise of bureaucratic discretion extremely inefficient. They paint a picture of government agencies grinding to a halt under the onslaught of consultations, investigations, and appeals. Examples of the costs and inefficiencies associated with the administration of unemployment insurance, immigration policy, and income assistance programs are not hard to find. On the other hand, striking a balance between efficiency and fairness has proved notoriously difficult. Case 5.2 raises

---

CASE 5.2
THE PATTERN IS OBVIOUS

Sandra, an investigator for the Workmen's Compensation Board, is discussing a report which she recently submitted to Bill, her supervisor.

Bill: I've been looking over this recommendation for Mrs. Brown. You want to suspend her widow's pension.

Sandra: Yes, she's a prostitute. According to the rules, she's been leading "an immoral and improper life" and therefore she is not eligible for benefits.

Bill: Are you really sure she's a hooker, Sandra? That's difficult to prove. The evidence in your report just isn't good enough. It's mostly third hand – you rely on reports by the neighbours that she was seen entering her home with a male friend and a case of beer. Big deal! So she spends time at the Legion? So do a lot of other people, and that doesn't make them prostitutes.

Sandra: Look, Bill, the rules say if she's a hooker, she's not eligible for benefits. I'm convinced that she's a prostitute.

Bill: Sandra, you're a good investigator, and I respect your judgment. If you say she's a prostitute, then I believe you. But frankly, the evidence you've got is simply insufficient to justify taking away her pension.

ISSUES

– Is Sandra justified in trying to take away Mrs. Brown's pension?

– If a decision is correct but defects in the reasoning process make it suspect, is that decision essentially unfair?

– Has fairness become a barrier to efficiency and effectiveness in the public service?

---

questions about procedural fairness and the trade-off between fairness and efficiency.

In sharp contrast with those who argue that procedural fairness can easily get out of hand are those who argue that it doesn't go far enough. Their most significant concern is that procedural fairness, as generally defined by the courts and ombudsmen, does little to make the duty of fairness meaningful to a significant part of the public. In essence, they argue that "the structures and processes normally regarded as components of 'good' administration are consistently weighted against the less advantaged... Disadvantaged individuals only have their powerlessness and alienation reinforced when attempting to deal with bureaucracy and its formal processes."[38]

The antidote to this situation is to widen the duty of fairness to make it more proactive. Instead of waiting for the public to come to them, public servants should be required to seek out and consult individuals who are likely to be affected by an action of government or are eligible for certain services, helping them to articulate their needs or concerns and gain access to relevant programs.[39] Instead of standardizing services, public servants should be "tailoring" them to fit the needs of newly identified groups of clients. Finally, public servants should be obligated to build wide citizen participation into policy-making in order to ensure that everyone whose rights might be affected by a decision is not just "allowed" to participate in the decision, but supported in so doing. Overall, the thrust of this movement is to extend the meaning of the duty of fairness to include a strong obligation to ensure accessibility, consultation, participation, and responsiveness. This duty was foreshadowed in chapter 2 in the discussion of the procedural approach to defining the public interest. We shall see in chapter 7 that defining the duty of fairness in this way also has powerful implications for the accountability of public servants.

Incorporating obligations such as these into the duty of service to the public raises the blood pressure of those concerned that increases in fairness inevitably come at the expense of efficiency and effectiveness. The essence of their concern has been expressed as follows:

> Consultations with individual citizens, citizens' groups and advisory bodies can be extremely time-consuming and consequently, an inefficient use of the time and energy of government officials. Such consultations can also lead to less efficient and effective government by causing delays in the making of decisions and the delivery of programmes. Efficiency and effectiveness can be further reduced if "expert" public servants are obliged to take undue account of the views of "amateur" citizens.[40]

As noted earlier, the response by the advocates of fairness is that far from being incompatible or mutually exclusive, fairness, efficiency, and effectiveness are mutually dependent. Improved access, consultation, participation, and responsiveness lead to more appropriate

---

CASE 5.3
HOW MUCH TALK IS ENOUGH?

Paul and Dean are employees in a city planning office. They disagree over what groups should be consulted about a proposed new development in the downtown area of their city.

Paul: I think the proposed new development of the downtown core is going to be great. It's really going to revitalize those two blocks. I'm anxious to let the developers get started on it.

Dean: I think you're right. The mayor seems keen, too. We'll need some public input on this, though.

Paul: Yeah, I guess so. But I think we should really be selective about whom we consult – just the businesses in the immediate area of the project. They're the ones who will really be affected by this development.

Dean: I don't agree. I think we have an obligation to search out other interested parties and ask them for their input. After all, we are altering the whole character of the downtown area. It's not just a few nearby businesses that will be affected.

Paul: Public participation takes forever. If we let everyone in the city look at the plans for this project it will never get off the ground. Besides, the mayor and city council have approved the project in principle, and the public do elect them to run the city and make decisions like this. Let's move this participation activity along and let the developers get on with it. If we do it your way we'll just delay the project unnecessarily.

ISSUES

– Is Paul justified in limiting public participation on the grounds of efficiency? Is he being unfair by not wanting to consult the general public?

– Is it fair to the businesses in the immediate area of the project to weigh their input equally with that of other interests?

– How do you keep proactive consultation from becoming too political?

---

allocations of resources, the co-operation of the affected community, and a reduction in costly *ex post facto* struggles against arbitrary decision-making.

Last, but possibly most important, fears have also been expressed about the potential for the politicization of the bureaucracy inherent in this expanded duty to enhance fairness. The concern here is the degree to which the more exposed role of public servants will offend the conventions of political neutrality and ministerial responsibility. As Hodgetts notes, "if this situation becomes the norm rather than the exception we are likely to find a great deal less permanency in the public service."[41] It is not clear if the more proactive public servant can avoid straying into the territory traditionally reserved for politicians.

Case 5.3 examines the issue of public participation in the decision-making process. If we accept the notion that public servants have a duty to ensure that all interests are fairly represented in the development of policy, then the appropriate extent of participation must be defined clearly. Neither unilateral decision-making by public servants nor an exhaustive participative process is desirable. The former appears arbitrary, while the latter may impede efficiency. Moreover, every effort must be made to clarify the line between administrative consultation and political decision-making.

Conclusion

Many observers are pessimistic about the prospects of building a duty of service to the public firmly into the administrative culture of the public sector. But there may be an even more fundamental barrier to the development of a service-to-the-public ethic in government. Is it realistic to expect public servants to embrace the notion of service as if they worked for McDonalds? Transactions between the citizen and the state are not often like the buyer-seller relationship in the private sector. In the public sector the client is more often than not a supplicant. Moreover, there is no competition! Can the incentives be changed? Can the duty of service to the public be built more securely into the administrative culture and the value systems of individual public servants? If not, the main incentive driving the public servant in this context will remain fear: fear of the exposure of inefficiency or ineffectiveness by the government auditor, and fear of the exposure of unfair procedure by the ombudsman. Fear hardly seems an adequate foundation for so fundamental a duty.

Notes

1. York Wilbern, "Types and Levels of Public Morality," in Elizabeth K. Kellar, ed., *Ethical Insight, Ethical Action: Perspectives for the Local Government Manager* (Washington: ICMA, 1988), p. 15.

2. See David Zussman, "The Image of the Public Service in Canada," *Canadian Public Administration* 25 (Spring 1982), pp. 63-80.

3. Institute of Public Administration of Canada, *Statement of Principles Regarding the Conduct of Public Employees* (Toronto: Institute of Public Administration of Canada, 1986). See Appendix.

4. See M.D. Bayles, *Professional Ethics* (Belmont, California: Wadsworth Publishing Company, 1981), ch. 4, for a fuller discussion of the nature of the obligation of the professional to the client.

5. Report of the Task Force on Service to the Public, February 2, 1981 (unpublished), pp. II-2 and 3.

6. Treasury Board of Canada, *Principles for the Management of the Public Service of Canada* (Ottawa: Supply and Services Canada, 1983), p. 6.

7. *Governing Values* (Ottawa: Supply and Services Canada, 1987), pp. 17, 20.,

8. The Corporation of the District of West Vancouver, "Statement of Organizational Philosophy," August, 1985.

9. Government of Ontario, Human Resources Secretariat, *Focus on . . .*, 1986.

10. "A Code of Conduct and Ethics for the Public Service of Alberta," s. 1.

11. Corporate Communications Branch, Corporation of the City of Ottawa, "Service Improvement: Doing a Good Job Better," n.d.

12. Organization for Economic Cooperation and Development, *Administration as Service* (Paris: OECD Publications, 1986), p. 131.

13. See *Report of the Auditor General of Canada to the House of Commons for the Fiscal Year Ended 31 March, 1988* (Ottawa: Supply and Services Canada, 1988), ch. 4.

14. See, for example, Peter Wilenski, "Social Change as a Source of Competing Values in Public Administration," *Australian Journal of Public Administration* 47 (September 1988), pp. 213-21.

15. For an example of how the public service "vision" is being translated into reality, see Syd Minuk, "The City of Calgary: A Service Improvement Strategy," *Tapping the Network Journal* (Winter 1988), pp. 6-8.

16. See Charles Gilbert, "The Framework of Administrative Responsibility," *Journal of Politics* 21 (August 1959), pp. 373-407; Kenneth Kernaghan, "Changing Concepts of Power and Responsibility in the Canadian Public Service," *Canadian Public Administration* 21 (Fall 1978), pp. 389-406; and Bruce Rawson, "The Responsibility of the Public Servant to the Public: Accessibility, Fairness and Efficiency," *Canadian Public Administration* 27 (Winter 1984), pp. 601-10.

17. See Paul M. Dubois, *Modern Administrative Practices in Human Services* (Springfield: Charles C. Thomas, 1981), esp. ch. 10.

18. Bayles, *Professional Ethics*, p. 19.

19. H.G. Frederickson and D.K. Hart, "The Public Service and the Patriotism of Benevolence," *Public Administration Review* 45 (September/October 1985), pp. 548-49.

20. *Governing Values*, p. 17.

21. Peter A. French, *Ethics in Government* (Englewood Cliffs, N.J.: Prentice Hall, 1983), p. 142.

22. Terry L. Cooper, *The Responsible Administrator* (Port Washington, N.Y.: Kennikat Press, 1982), p. 39.

23. Peter Wilenski, *Public Power and Public Administration* (Sydney: Hale and Iremonger, 1986), pp. 158-59.

24. See Mark Moore, "Realms of Obligation and Virtue," in Joel L. Fleishman et al., eds., *Public Duties: The Moral Obligations of Government Officials* (Cambridge, Mass.: Harvard University Press, 1981), pp. 21-23.

25. The most obvious driving force behind this redefinition is T.J. Peters and R.H. Waterman, *In Search of Excellence: Lessons from American's Best Run Companies* (New York: Harper and Row, 1982).

26. See, for instance, Harold W. Williams, "In Search of Bureaucratic Excellence," *The Bureaucrat* 15 (Spring 1986), pp. 16-21.

27. See J. Cutt, "Accountability, Efficiency, and the 'Bottom Line' in Non-Profit Organizations," *Canadian Public Administration* 25 (Fall 1982), pp. 311-31; and Walter L. Balk, "Toward a Government Productivity Ethic," *The Bureaucrat* 38 (January/February 1978), pp. 46-50.

28. A.W. Johnson, "Efficiency in Government and Business," *Canadian Public Administration* 6 (September 1963), pp. 249-50.

29. See Daniel Katz et al., *Bureaucratic Encounters: A Pilot Study in the Evaluation of Government Services*, (Ann Arbor: Institute for Social Research, 1975), ch. 5.

30. See Christopher Hodgkinson, *Towards a Philosophy of Administration* (Oxford: Basil Blackwell, 1978), especially ch. 11.

31. Ralph P. Hummel, *The Bureaucratic Experience* (New York: St. Martins, 1977), p. 22.

32. See David P. Fauri, "Public Service as a Service to Clients," *American Behavioral Scientist* 21 (July/August 1978), pp. 859-79. Some observers argue that the bureaucratic culture is even antithetical to competence. See J. Hall and S. Donnell, "The Quiet Crisis in Government," *The Bureaucrat* 14 (Summer 1985), pp. 39-45.

33. Mark R. Yessian, "Delivering Service in a Rapidly Changing Public Sector," *American Behavioral Scientist* 21 (July/August, 1978), p. 844. See also W. Bennis, *Beyond Bureaucracy: Essays on the Development and Evolution of Human Organization* (New York: McGraw Hill, 1973); and Peter Drucker, "New Templates for Today's Organizations," *Harvard Business Review* 52 (January/February, 1974), pp. 45-53.

34. Yessian, "Delivering Service," pp. 845-46.

35. See Tom R. Tyler, "What is Procedural Justice?: Criteria Used by Citizens to Assess the Fairness of Legal Procedures," *Law and Society Review* 22, no. 1 (1988), pp. 131-32; and Elaine B. Sharp, "Citizen Perception of Police Service Delivery: A Look at Some Consequences," *Policy Studies Journal* 9 (Summer 1981), pp. 971-79.

36. Gillian Andrews, "What Is Administrative Law," *Newsletter*, Legal Resource Centre, Vancouver, B.C. (1981), p. 4.

37. Terry Cooper raises the issue of the tendency of the values of fairness and efficiency to lead to standardization of service. Cooper, *The Responsible Administrator*, pp. 39-41.

38. Wilenski, *Public Power*, p. 160.

39. See John P. Burke, *Bureaucratic Responsibility* (Baltimore: Johns Hopkins University Press, 1986), ch. 11.

40. Kenneth Kernaghan, "Evolving Patterns of Administrative Responsiveness to the Public," *International Review of Administrative Sciences* 52 (March 1986), p. 13.

41. J. E. Hodgetts, "Bureaucratic Initiatives, Citizen Involvement, and the Quest for Administrative Accountability," *Transactions of the Royal Society of Canada*, Series IV, vol. 12 (1974), p. 236.

Chapter 6

Conflict of Interest

Conflict of interest is one of the most common forms of unethical conduct in the public service. It is certainly the type that is best known to the general public and that arouses the most controversy outside government. Conflicts of interest are pervasive in society and they affect business and voluntary organizations as well as government organizations. However, this chapter is concerned solely with conflicts of interest in government. The focus is primarily on public servants but lessons are drawn also from the experience of politicians.

What *is* a conflict of interest? How can the public servant's duty to avoid conflicts of interest be fulfilled? How can a real conflict of interest be distinguished from an apparent conflict and from a potential conflict? Why should we be concerned about conflicts of interest? What are the various forms of conflict of interest? These are the major questions considered in this chapter.

Defining the Duty

It is important to define the term conflict of interest because there is much disagreement and confusion about its meaning. A conflict of interest can be defined as a situation in which a public official has a private or personal interest sufficient to influence or to appear to influence the objective exercise of his or her official duties.[1] Similarly, a conflict of interest is said to exist "when the private interests of an individual are at variance with his or her official duties and responsibilities to the government."[2] Other definitions relate conflict of interest to the broad issue of acting in the public interest which was discussed in chapter 2; one means by which public servants can avoid conflicts of interest is by putting the public interest before private benefit. The government of Manitoba asserts that the guidelines in its Conflict of Interest Policy "aim at safeguarding the public interest. Stated simply, the intent is to prevent employees from using, or appearing to use, public office for private gain."

The Conflict of Interest Guidelines for Saskatchewan public service employees capture the essence of conflict of interest in the following definition:

> A conflict of interest is any situation in which a public employee, either for himself/herself or some other person(s), attempts to promote a private or personal interest which results or appears to result in the following:
>   (i) an interference with the objective exercise of his/her duties in the public service
>   (ii) a gain or an advantage by virtue of his/her position in the public service.

The Statement of Principles of the Institute of Public Administration of Canada reflects these several definitions by providing that "public employees should not engage in any business or transaction or have any financial or other personal interest that is, or may appear to be, incompatible with the performance of their official duties."

There are several complications in defining the public servant's duty to avoid conflict of interest. First, there are many variations of conflict of interest, ranging from influence-peddling, which is prohibited by the criminal code, to such activities as improper use of government property, moonlighting, and accepting benefits. As a result, many public servants are genuinely perplexed as to whether certain activities constitute conflicts of interest. Precisely what kinds of business involvement are incompatible with one's official duties? Can government property be used to assist an organization like the Red Cross? What forms of outside employment are permissible? The ethical rules set out by some governments are too vague to provide much practical guidance on such questions, but other governments specify in considerable detail the forbidden types of conflict of interest and provide hypothetical examples of each. In the area of accepting benefits, for example, the Conflict of Interest Guidelines for Saskatchewan public service employees not only set out criteria to define outside employment (e.g., self-employment, activities from which there is a monetary reward) but also provide examples of activities which are considered to be outside employment (e.g., farming, freelance journalism, consulting work).

A second complication is that the interpretation of conflict of interest rules varies not only from one government and one department to another but also from one public servant to another. The 1988 Code of Conduct of the City of Toronto provided that, to avoid conflicts of interest, "management and professional employees [should] not be allowed to appear" before council, its committees or other civic agencies "other than in the performance of their duties." The leader of a union local described this regulation as "a gag rule" which would "muzzle the free speech of thousands of employees who work for local government."[3] A closely related complication is that opinions as to what activities constitute conflict of interest change over time. For example, dual employment by public servants is generally more permissible than it used to be.

A final complication is the difficulty of distinguishing a *real* conflict of interest from an *apparent* conflict and from a *potential* conflict. This important issue is considered separately below.

Real, Apparent, or Potential Conflict?

Many public officials are involved in conflict of interest situations in the normal course of carrying out their official responsibilities. In most cases, however, their involvement is in an apparent or a potential conflict of interest rather than in a real conflict. The wrongdoing lies not in mere involvement in a conflict of interest situation but in not taking the necessary steps to avoid a real conflict. The Parker Commission noted that "at least three prerequisites have to be established before a public office holder can be said to be in a position of *real* conflict of interest. They are: the existence of a private interest; that it is known to the public office holder; and that it has a connection or nexus with his or her public duties or responsibilities that is sufficient to influence the exercise of those duties or responsibilities."[4]

An *apparent* conflict of interest is one which is deduced from appearances. The Parker Commission asserted that "an apparent conflict of interest exists when there is a reasonable apprehension, which reasonably well-informed persons could properly have, that a conflict of interest exists."[5] For example, a public servant who awards contracts to a firm which employs one of his or her relatives may appear to be involved in a conflict of interest even though there is no actual wrongdoing. Justice Mahoney of the Federal Court of Canada has provided the following test for determining the existence of apparent conflicts of interest: "Would an informed person, viewing the matter realistically and practically and having thought the matter through, think it more likely than not that the public servant, whether consciously or unconsciously, will be influenced in the performance of his official duties by considerations having to do with his private interests?"[6]

A *potential* conflict of interest is one which may develop into an actual conflict. The Parker Commission explains that "the potential for conflict exists as soon as the public office holder can foresee that he or she has a private economic interest that may be sufficient to influence a public duty or responsibility. As soon as a real conflict of interest is foreseeable, the public office holder must take all appropriate steps to extricate himself or herself from the predicament." The commission notes further that "if the caution signs are ignored and the public office holder proceeds to discharge any duty or responsibility of the particular public office that could affect or be affected by the private interest, the line is crossed and a situation of real conflict ensues."[7] For example, a public servant who is in a position to influence the fate of grant applications from a firm in which he or she holds shares, has a potential conflict of interest.

Each allegation or possibility of conflict of interest must be considered carefully in the light of the explanations provided above. Cases 6.1 and 6.2 are designed partly to provide practice in determining what kind of conflict, if any, is involved.

It is common in popular discussions to view conflicts of interest as including only those situations in which public office has actually been used for personal economic or financial gain. The Parker Commission, for example, defines a real conflict of interest as a situation in which a public office-holder "has knowledge of a private *economic* interest that is sufficient to influence the exercise of his or her public duties and responsibilities."[8] The term is often interpreted more broadly, however, to refer to the use of public office for any kind of private or personal gain. Thus, for example, a public servant may gain in popularity rather than in the pocketbook by appointing friends or relatives to government posts. Similarly, a public servant who passes along confidential information which friends and relatives can use to their economic advantage may achieve no personal economic benefit. An immigration officer who promises special treatment to an immigrant in return for sexual favours receives no financial benefit. Conflict of interest may even be interpreted to include the use of public office for partisan gain. Consider, for example, the case of a public servant who provides confidential information to an opposition political party in order to enhance his or her personal partisan objectives. Finally, the term conflict of interest may be extended to conflict between one's official duties and conduct in one's private life. An example of this type of conflict is the social worker who beats his wife.

Despite the broad interpretation which can be given to the term conflict of interest, it must be acknowledged that most conflicts which attract public attention involve economic benefits for public officials. Moreover, it is much easier to discern and to regulate economic benefits than those of an emotional or psychological nature.

It is sometimes argued that a person can only be said to be in a real conflict of interest position if he or she actually benefits from the situation. Thus it is sometimes argued, erroneously in our view, that public officials who try, without success, to use their public office for private gain are not guilty of wrongdoing. This is the argument presented by Sinclair Stevens, the former federal minister of regional and industrial expansion, who was deemed by the Parker Commission to have been involved in fourteen real conflicts of interest. Counsel for Mr. Stevens argued that real conflict of interest should be restricted to those instances where a public official has "actually made a decision that conferred a benefit. According to this definition, a minister of the Crown who met with a party that was clearly seeking government work from the minister, and who discussed with that party a private proposal that would further the minister's personal interests, would not be in a position of conflict unless he or she actually decided to award government work to that party."[9] The commission rejected this definition as unduly narrow. A key consideration here is that the public official is actively seeking to advance his or her personal interests.

The penalty imposed on public servants who fail in efforts to seek private advantage from their public office will usually be less than for those who succeed; the fact remains, however, that even the attempt to secure such benefits constitutes misconduct. Are we likely to have any more trust in public officials who fail rather than succeed in their efforts to use their public office for personal enrichment?

There is also disagreement over the importance that should be attached to apparent conflicts of interest. Is it appropriate in some instances to answer conflict of interest allegations with the argument that what may appear to some people to be a conflict really is not? Or is the threat to public trust and confidence in government so important that even the appearance of conflict must be removed? Consider the case of meteorologists working for the Atmospheric Environment Service of the federal Department of the Environment.10 Some radio stations like to employ such meteorologists outside their working hours to provide weather forecasts. The department tends to look favourably upon such off-duty work because it means that the public receives weather forecasts from trained meteorologists. However, off-duty meteorologists, especially if they are supervisors, may receive or may appear to receive preferential treatment from their co-workers in the government weather office when they are preparing their weather broadcasts. Where does the public interest lie in such circumstances?

It is important to recognize, especially with the growing emphasis on avoiding even apparent and potential conflicts of interest, that some definitions of what constitutes a conflict have become very broad, perhaps unduly so. Note, for example, the interpretations by the Parker Commission explained earlier. This expansion of the definition is accompanied by much uncertainty among public servants, including public service managers, as to what is a conflict and what is not. We shall see in chapter 8 that there has been a corresponding expansion in the number of statutes, regulations, and guidelines designed to deter and punish conflicts.

Why are We Concerned about Conflicts of Interest?

It is sometimes suggested that concern about conflicts of interest is a luxury in the sense that we have, in western democratic countries, cleaned up the worst forms of corruption and can now focus on comparatively mild forms of misconduct, including the appearance of and the potential for misconduct. Conflict of interest can be viewed as "a matter that only an otherwise secure and established society can afford to worry about. Only when grosser larcenies in government have been reduced to tolerable limits – only when overt venality is uncommon enough to shock – is it possible for a government to concentrate on potential for evil and try to head off corruption at its sources."[11] It is often suggested also that compared to the shocking level of corruption in some Third World countries, the concern about conflicts of interest in developed countries such as Canada and the United States is indeed a luxury.

Since the Second World War the level of corruption surrounding many governments in the western world has significantly diminished, in part because of the increase in laws, regulations, and guidelines forbidding the use of public office for private gain. But can governments in Canada afford to treat conflict of interest as a luxury item to which resources only occasionally need to be devoted? Politicians and public servants whose careers have been critically affected by involvement – or allegations of involvement – in conflict of interest would answer no. So, it appears, would members of the general public.

In fact, a primary reason for concern about conflicts of interest is that they reduce public trust and confidence in the integrity and impartiality of government. In this respect, the appearance of a conflict can be as damaging as an actual conflict. Whether members of the public are motivated by genuine commitment to high ethical standards in government or by envy of those in a position to benefit from conflicts of interest, there is no doubt that public expectations regarding the ethical standards of government officials have become much higher over the last two decades. This public concern has been stimulated by media coverage of instances and allegations of conflict of interest, which in turn have prompted many politicians to seek out cases of actual or apparent conflicts of interest involving their political opponents with a view to using adverse media coverage for political advantage. Some journalists and politicians have been reckless and irresponsible in their allegations against government officials, but others have exposed and publicized serious ethical offenses.

Increased concern in contemporary society about conflicts of interest has come about in large part from the realization that public servants now have more opportunities to put private benefit before public duty. These opportunities arise from the increased scale and complexity of government and the expansion of bureaucratic power in the policy process. Public concern has been accompanied by changed attitudes toward some of the variations of conflicts of interest discussed below. For example, the practice of moonlighting has become more permissible, while post-employment practices have become more tightly regulated. It can be argued that over the past two decades public servants have been given greater motivation to become involved in real or apparent conflicts of interest. The slowing of growth in government means that public servants now have fewer opportunities for promotion and that their jobs are likely to be less permanent. The detrimental effect of these developments on morale has been aggravated by the relatively low public image of the public service. It is not surprising then that more public servants should feel less committed to their job and that they should increasingly engage in activities for remuneration outside government as a hedge against losing or quitting their job. In some cases, public servants may feel that the financial and psychic rewards from serving the public are so inadequate that they are justified in using their public office for private gain.

The revelation of even a few conflict of interest offenses is important because the publicity they receive can have a negative effect on public trust and confidence in government that is way out of proportion to their number and gravity. Given the low public regard in which many members of the public hold government officials, there is an inclination to conclude that the few offenses that are revealed are only the tip of the iceberg. The news media tend to give more publicity to conflicts of interest involving politicians than those involving public servants. But the reputation of public servants suffers along with that of politicians as a result of the spillover effect on appointed officials of the ethical offenses of elected officials. Is it reasonable to expect high ethical performance by public servants when elected officials, especially cabinet ministers, do not provide a role model worthy of emulation?

A former senior public servant, whose experience was that "nearly all" of the many ministers under whom he worked were "meticulous and upright," provided the following anecdote about one who was not.

... Another minister was angry with me because I returned a case of wine or spirits that had been sent to me by someone in the business who might have asked a favour of the government with which it was negotiating for support. The minister was not about to send back the cases of wine he had received. I had to advise him that I felt bound to record my disapproval. He was furious because the files would contain the evidence of his indiscretion. Although he failed to have the evidence removed, he kept his prizes and wasn't publicly discovered. The industry got what it was after, I should add.[12]

The foregoing arguments are based largely on utilitarian considerations in that they focus on the consequences of public servants' involvement in conflicts of interest. The deontological approach, which focuses on the nature of the act rather than on the consequences, heightens concern about such involvement. It prompts us to ask whether we would accept the notion of everyone engaging in conflicts of interest. Moreover, from behind a "veil of ignorance," would we condone conflicts of interest if we didn't know whether we would ever be in a position to benefit from one?

Variations on a Common Theme

Continuing problems in the conflict-of-interest sphere arise in part from the fact that there are so many variations of conflict of interest. It is useful to depict each variation on a separate continuum running from "black" conflicts through various shades of grey to "off-white" conflicts. For example, the variation known as accepting benefits ranges along the continuum from bribery through the acceptance of gifts or entertainment of varying but substantial value to the acceptance of benefits of nominal value. Other types of conflict of interest, for example, moonlighting, are usually grey-area conflicts which normally do not approach the black pole of the continuum. It is notable also that as the seriousness of offenses move them toward the black pole, a decision has to be made as to whether the offense should be handled within the government as an administrative infraction or treated as a violation of criminal law. For example, public servants may simply be reprimanded for accepting benefits of slightly more than nominal value, but they may be prosecuted under the criminal code for accepting a large bribe.

Conflicts of interest can be divided into the following eight categories: self-dealing, accepting benefits, influence-peddling, using government property, using confidential information, outside employment, post-employment, and personal conduct. Some of these categories require lengthier treatment than others because of the comparative difficulty of defining and regulating them.

The first three of these variations of conflict of interest are similar in that they involve situations where public servants use their public office to bring about decisions which favour themselves, their family, or an organization in which they have an interest.

Self-dealing

Self-dealing refers to a situation where one takes an action in an official capacity which involves dealing with oneself in a private capacity and which confers a benefit on oneself. In recent years, the notion of self has been expanded to include one's spouse, family members, and business partners. An obvious example of self-dealing is a public servant who awards a contract to a company which he or she owns. In an actual case, a federal public servant admitted that in his capacity as the chief of security services for the Department of the Secretary of State he had rented electronic surveillance equipment from a firm in which he was a partner.[13] Consider whether any of the participants in case 6.1 are involved in a conflict of interest.

Accepting Benefits

As noted above, the acceptance of benefits can take the form of bribery at the one extreme and the receipt of benefits of nominal value at the other. A wide range of benefits can be conferred on public servants, including gifts, meals, free travel, paid vacations, entertainment, and money.

The IPAC Statement of Principles asserts that "public employees should not solicit nor, unless duly authorized, accept transfers of economic value from persons with whom they have contact in their official capacity." This principle suggests the desirability of providing specific guidelines regarding the acceptance of benefits. Accepting benefits which are of such magnitude that the fitting response is prosecution under the criminal code are comparatively easy to handle.

CASE 6.1
ALL IN THE FAMILY

The following conversation takes place between two middle managers in a provincial Department of Regional Industrial Expansion.

Mike: I understand that you've had a request for financial assistance from a computer manufacturer.

Frances: We've been flooded with requests lately, Mike. This has been a bad year for this province. But I think I know the company you mean. It's in Spruceville, isn't it?

Mike: Yes, that's the one. They've been in touch with me, and apparently they're in a real crisis situation. Frankly, Frances, they're afraid that they'll have to shut down if they don't get some financial help soon.

Frances: That doesn't sound good. But I just received their application this week. With the pile of applications on my desk right now, it'll be another month or two at least before I get to it.

Mike: That'll be too late. The owner of the firm is married to my sister, so I told him I'd look into the situation. I think their financial situation is critical enough to justify putting their application near the top of the pile.

ISSUES

– Is Mike in a real, apparent, or potential conflict of interest situation here?

– Is the firm's reported dire financial situation a sufficient justification for Mike to involve himself in the application vetting process?

– How should Frances respond to Mike's request?

– How would the average citizen react to this situation?

– Would the case be handled any differently if Mike was not related to the owner of the firm?

– Should information about the firm's critical financial situation be ignored because of the source of the information?

The real difficulty comes with benefits that fall into the grey area, such as meals associated with a business meeting, a bottle of liquor at Christmas time, an evening at the theatre, an honorarium for a speech, or a gift which may be perceived as having more than nominal value. The nature of the problem can be illuminated by the efforts of governments to regulate the acceptance of benefits. An informal guideline which is reported to have existed in earlier and simpler times was that public servants should accept only gifts which they could consume within a twenty-four-hour period. A guideline so geared to individual capacity was probably never appropriate; it would certainly be considered inappropriate today. What mechanism should be devised to handle cases like the following? A developer reported that "shortly after New Year's Eve two years ago, he met a senior regional official at a liquor store at the opposite end of the region. He said the red-faced official was cashing in two trolley carts full of liquor that he had received as gifts."[14]

Is the best solution to prohibit the receipt of gifts of any kind? This approach has the virtue of simplicity but is it sensible and feasible? Most governments permit the receipt of casual benefits such as small gifts or hospitality. For example, the Code of Conduct and Ethics for the Public Service of Alberta provides that "an employee shall not accept a gift, favour or service from an individual, organization or corporation, other than: the normal exchange of gifts between friends; the normal exchange of hospitality between persons doing business together; tokens exchanged as part of protocol; or the normal presentation of gifts to persons participating in public functions."

Some governments try to define what "nominal" value means by setting a limit of, say, one hundred dollars. Is this limit too high or too low? What constitutes a benefit of nominal value? Public servants involved in certain commercial or diplomatic activities with persons from foreign countries where the giving of gifts is normal practice would have genuine problems with a limit of one hundred, or even two hundred dollars. Compare the situation of a public servant from the Business Development Bank who is invited to dine at the home of a business person seeking a loan to that of a public servant from the Department of External Affairs who is invited to dine at the embassy home of a foreign diplomat whose country is seeking a loan. Should the rules on accepting benefits be tailored to the public servant's level and responsibilities in the public service? Could the same objective be achieved by requiring due authorization from administrative or political superiors before any benefits are accepted? The Code of Conduct for Employees of the Metropolitan Corporation of Toronto provides that even sporadic or casual benefits such as small gifts or entertainment should be accepted only with the knowledge and consent of administrative superiors. The federal Conflict of Interest and Post-Employment Code for Public Office Holders provides that public servants who receive benefits worth two hundred dollars or more, "other than a gift, hospitality or other benefit from a family member or close friend, must notify the Assistant Deputy Registrar General and make a public declaration supplying adequate detail to identify the benefit, the donor, and the circumstances under which the benefit was received." But what about a government purchasing agent who accepts many gifts, none of which is valued at more than two hundred dollars? And what about public servants whose influence can be bought for the price of an expensive dinner?

Influence Peddling

Influence peddling is the practice of soliciting some form of benefit from individuals or organizations in exchange for the exercise of one's official authority or influence on their behalf. It is closely related to the practice of accepting benefits. However, it is a more active form of conflict of interest in that it involves the *solicitation* of benefits. Note that the IPAC principle quoted in the previous section provides that public servants should not *solicit* or *accept* benefits.

Using Government Property

The IPAC Statement of Principles provides specifically that "public employees should not use, or permit the use of, government property of any kind for activities not associated with the performance of their official duties, unless they are authorized to do so." The private use of government property can take a multitude of forms. It can range from relatively minor offenses such as taking pencils home or using a government office for non-government purposes to major offenses such as using government computers for a private business. It is notable, for example, that a federal public servant in Statistics Canada was disciplined not only for doing work for a private business on government time but also for using Statistics Canada's computer services in connection with that business.[15]

An absolute prohibition on the use of government property for private purposes is, like an absolute ban on accepting benefits, an administratively convenient approach; it is not necessarily, however, the most sensible one. It is for this reason that the IPAC principle contains the qualification "unless they are authorized to do so." This approach permits public servants to seek permission to use government property for private purposes in such exceptional circumstances as providing space for a Red Cross blood drive or a United Appeal fund drive. The important point here is that government property not be used for personal gain. But how far should this restriction be carried? Is it appropriate for municipal employees to take home from a department of public works yard scrap lumber which would otherwise be burned? Should the same opportunity be made available to the general public?

Using Confidential Information

What is involved here is the use for personal or private purposes of a particular form of government property, namely confidential information. The offense lies in using information, including information about decisions made by other public servants, for private gain. We have already learned from chapter 4 that there are serious consequences for public servants who disclose without authorization confidential government information. The consequences are likely to be even more serious if the information is used for the private benefit, especially for the economic benefit, of the public servants or their friends and relatives.

The IPAC Statement of Principles provides that "public employees should not seek or obtain personal or private gain from the use of information acquired during the course of their official duties which is not generally available to the public." For example, a federal public servant was dismissed because he borrowed money on the basis of "insider knowledge" and then invested that money in a company almost two weeks before information about a large government grant to the company was made available to the general public.[16] It follows, of course, that information made generally available to the public can be used by public servants with impunity. But does this really create an equitable situation for public servants and the general public with respect to the use of government information? Is it not possible, for example, for public servants to take advantage of advance information by accumulating funds which they can invest immediately upon the public announcement of a government contract for a particular firm? This kind of activity is difficult to regulate.

Should we worry less about such insider trading than about other kinds of conflict of interest because the benefits to the public servant cost the taxpayer nothing? How concerned should we be about a Department of Agriculture employee who uses statistics collected on crops to speculate on grain futures before these statistics are released to the public? To what extent is our concern about such behaviour motivated by envy and to what extent is it motivated by the need to preserve public confidence in the integrity of public officials?

Outside Employment

Outside employment, or moonlighting, refers to the work or activity in which a person engages outside normal working hours for additional remuneration. While such activity may be conducted on a full-time basis (for example, driving a taxi for a full shift each evening), it usually involves part-time work and includes a wide range of activities such as working for a non-governmental organization (for example, a business or an educational institution), running a business, or consulting.

Among the benefits to the employer claimed for moonlighting are better employee morale, less frustrated employees, increased skill development, and lower turnover rates.[17] Conflict of interest problems arise when the moonlighting activities of public servants clash with the performance of their official duties. More specifically, moonlighting may need to be restricted:

- if the activity is in direct competition with the employer;
- if the employee's work performance is affected;
- if the employer's property is being used to engage in the activity;
- if confidential information is being used by the employee;
- if the employee is using his/her position to solicit business; or
- if the employee's activity could be perceived by the public to be a conflict of interest.[18]

There are some obvious links between conflict of interest in the moonlighting sphere and other types of conflict, especially the use of

---

CASE 6.2
BY THE LIGHT OF THE MOON

This conversation takes place between two middle managers in the federal government.

Manjeet: A group of four of us have decided to start a consulting company on the side to run seminars telling businessmen how to deal with government, and, in particular, how to get contracts from government.

Arlene: Who's involved?

Manjeet: Four public servants.

Arlene: And what exactly are you going to offer?

Manjeet: We'll outline the various contract regulations, rules, policies, procedures, restraints, and constraints affecting the process. We're also going to offer advice for maximizing opportunities to sell goods and services to the government.

Arlene: My goodness! Surely you know you're not allowed to use information acquired during the course of your public service employment in that way!

Manjeet: That's true only if the information we're providing is not generally available to the public. All the information we're planning to give out is readily available from the departments themselves if anyone bothers to ask for it.

ISSUES

– Are Manjeet and his colleagues involved in a conflict of interest? If so, is it a real, apparent, or potential conflict?

– Is the integrity of the contracting out process threatened by such an activity as this?

– Does the fact that the information they would be providing is available to the public alter your view of the case?

– How do you think this situation would be viewed by the average citizen?

---

government property, the use of confidential information, and influence-peddling. Moreover, the *appearance* of conflict is a common problem with respect to moonlighting activities. Case 6.2 provides a basis for assessing the virtues and disadvantages of moonlighting and for examining its links to other types of conflict. Consider also the case of a federal public servant working for the Department of Employment and Immigration as an employment counsellor.[19] The Public Service Staff Relations Board found that this public servant had contravened the federal conflict of interest guidelines by trying during normal office hours to sell vacuum cleaners to clients of the department, by persuading a client to provide cheap labour for the painting of his house, and by releasing information about a client to the police and threatening to release the same information to a welfare agency.

While it is generally acknowledged that the use of confidential information is unacceptable in the conduct of moonlighting activities, there is more debate about the use of information in the form of knowledge and experience which has been acquired on the job. Is there anything wrong with a public servant using knowledge of government structures and procedures in a part-time business? Does it make a difference if this knowledge is readily available to the public from the government? Examine case 6.2 in the light of these questions.

Post-Employment

Post-employment is sometimes described as subsequent employment or future employment. It constitutes a conflict of interest when public servants use, or appear to use, information and contacts acquired while in government to benefit themselves or others after they leave government. The federal Conflict of Interest and Post-Employment Code provides that "public office holders shall not act, after they leave public office, in such a manner as to take improper advantage of their previous office." There are several possibilities for wrongdoing here. After public servants move out of government, they may use confidential information for personal benefit through self-employment (for example, as a consultant) or they may use such information for the benefit of a private firm by which they are employed. Public servants may also benefit by receiving privileged access or preferential treatment from their former colleagues. Even before leaving government, public servants may try to enhance their prospects for profitable private employment by granting preferential treatment to certain firms or organizations. The practice of "switching sides" – that is, taking up employment in the private sector which involves working on a matter for which the public servant was responsible in his or her government position – is considered to be especially offensive.

In recent years, media coverage of several public servants who have moved to private sector jobs, notably in professional associations, has set off alarm bells about possible conflicts of interest. For example, the air administrator of the Canadian Air Transportation Administration of Transport Canada became the president and chief executive officer of the Air Transport Association of Canada; a deputy minister of forests in British Columbia became president of the Council of Forest Industries in that province; and an assistant deputy minister of mineral policy in the federal Department of Energy, Mines and Resources became managing director of the Mining Association of Canada.

Among the several variations of conflict of interest, the post-employment problem is one of the most difficult to regulate. The difficulty arises in large part from the fact that the persons being regulated are *former* public servants; once public servants have left the government, the range of penalties that the government can apply to them is more limited. As a result, governments try to discourage public servants from using their public office unethically (for example, through influence-peddling) to attract job offers in the first place. Some governments require that public servants report to their superiors any job offers they receive, especially from persons with whom they have, or have had, official business. In the federal government, ministers and public servants are responsible for ensuring that former public officials do not take advantage of their previous position.

Efforts are also made to discourage public servants from accepting a private sector job in which they hope to use their specialized public service knowledge to earn a high salary. A common disincentive is to prohibit public servants from engaging for a period of time (for example, one or two years) in any employment which would conflict, or appear to conflict, with their official responsibilities. This "cooling-off" period not only discourages public servants from leaving government in the first place; it also minimizes the value of confidential information which they possess and it reduces the likelihood of a private employer obtaining a comparative advantage from the use of such information.

The problem of distinguishing between confidential information and information in the form of knowledge and experience which was discussed in the context of moonlighting is also a central consideration here. Could a persuasive argument be made that public servants, like their private sector counterparts, have the right to move from one job to another on the basis of their competence and reputation? How can an appropriate balance be struck between the right of public servants to move between public and private sector employment and the need to prevent abuse of confidential information and preserve public trust in the integrity of public officials? An analysis of case 6.3 will provide useful practice in answering such questions.

CASE 6.3
THE INSIDE TRACK

The following conversation takes place between Natasha and Mario, two officials of the Ministry of Justice.

Natasha: What are we going to do about that new contract that's come up?

Mario: That work would have been Smith's responsibility.

Natasha: Yes, but she left us about a month ago and has returned to private law practice. Before she left, though, she developed a contracting-out process for programs of this kind.

Mario: Good. Have you received any bids?

Natasha: Yes, we have. Actually, we've received quite a few. In fact, one of the bids came from the law firm which Smith just joined.

Mario: Well then, that firm would seem to be the logical choice for handling this contract. Smith knows exactly what's expected and she knows all the players.

Natasha: Yeah, that's true, but it may not look so good giving the contract to someone who set up the process and worked here until a month ago.

Mario: Hell, are you suggesting that we have to exclude the best-qualified firm because one of their lawyers worked for us? Who'd work for the public service under those conditions?

ISSUES

– Would Mario be acting irresponsibly in hiring Smith's law firm?
– Is Smith in a conflict of interest situation?
– What limits should be placed on the relationship which an ex-public servant can have with his or her ex-department?
– Can you justify limiting the freedom of ex-public servants?

Personal Conduct

Is a public servant's personal life any of the government's business? Can a public servant be in a real or an apparent conflict of interest because of improper or questionable conduct in his or her private life? Could drug or alcohol addiction be deemed to be "a situation in which a public official has a private or personal interest sufficient to influence or to appear to influence the objective exercise of his or her official duties?" What about wife or child abuse? Does improper conduct have to become public knowledge before the public servant's administrative superiors can take official notice of it, or is it sufficient for administrative superiors simply to know that improper conduct has occurred?

The personal conduct of public servants is obviously an area where government must tread warily for fear of infringing on the public servants' right to privacy. We noted in chapter 4 that there are strong utilitarian and deontological arguments for individual privacy. But are public servants entitled to the same privacy as other citizens? Does the power which public servants exercise in the development and implementation of public policy justify greater concern about their personal conduct and greater encroachments on their privacy? Should we be more concerned about the conduct of elected than of appointed officials? Would that make sense when many public servants exercise more power in the public policy process than many elected officials, especially backbench legislators?

These are difficult and complicated questions; yet on occasion they must be answered. Certainly the sphere of personal conduct is likely to give rise to more disagreement than most other types of conflict of interest. It seems reasonable to argue that in at least two circumstances, a public servant's personal conduct, outside government, may constitute a conflict of interest. The first circumstance is when a public servant's conduct (for example, drug addiction) makes him or her vulnerable to pressure to use his or her public office improperly. The second circumstance is when the public servant's conduct brings significant discredit to the government or to a particular department and thereby undermines public trust in public officials. On the other hand, could a convincing case be made that the public and indeed the government only have a legitimate interest in the public servant's personal conduct in private life if that conduct actually affects adversely the performance of his or her official duties?

It has been argued that:

> ...if integrity is required of a public servant in the per-
> formance of his duties, the same requirement applies to his
> conduct in private life, particularly if he occupies a fairly
> high position in management. When a public servant in
> such a position engages in activities prohibited by law or
> considered of questionable morality by the general public,
> this constitutes an offense which in turn becomes...a
> breach of discipline liable to a sanction.[20]

Implicit in this argument is the suggestion that we should be more
concerned if a public servant who regularly engages in fist fights in a
local bar is a law enforcement officer than if he or she is a janitor.
Similarly, we should be more distressed if a public servant addicted to
drugs is a deputy minister than if he or she is a file clerk. In any event,
it is clear that each case of questionable or improper personal conduct
involving public servants needs to be carefully considered on its
merits.

Conclusion

At several points in this chapter, we have asserted or implied the need
for conflict of interest rules. These rules are designed to prevent real,
apparent, or potential conflicts of interest from arising and to provide a
basis for handling them when they do arise. The federal Task Force on
Conflict of Interest observed that "in an earlier time...the public was
more prepared to give the benefit of the doubt to a minister or public
official. In other words, there was confidence that such officials would
give precedence to their public duties over their private interests. This
is no longer so. The public has come to expect positive measures
designed to remove or minimize the conflict of interests."[21]

Governments across Canada at all levels have responded to this
desire for positive measures with an unprecedented number and
variety of conflict of interest rules. The form of these rules varies from
one jurisdiction to another and includes statutes, regulations, and
guidelines. Conflict of interest rules often form part of a code of ethics
or a conflict of interest code which prohibits the several forms of
conflict explained earlier in this chapter. Among the techniques used
are rules requiring divestment of one's assets and business con-
nections; the arrangement of a blind, frozen or retention trust for one's

assets; and disclosure of one's assets.[22] The utility of such rules and of codes of ethics in general is examined in chapter 8.

Clearly, there is a need for continuing vigilance to ensure that even a small number of public servants do not use their public office for private or personal gain. There is, however, legitimate concern that the rights of responsible public servants are sometimes unduly diminished by conflict of interest rules. This concern has grown over the past two decades as a result not only of the expanded scope and volume of the rules but also of the increased emphasis on removing apparent as well as real conflicts. While the need for public confidence in government requires that most apparent conflicts be removed, allegations of conflict occasionally flow from an excessive zeal. Those public servants who draft and enforce the rules should ask themselves whether they would want the same rules applied to themselves.

Notes

1. This definition is adapted from Kenneth Kernaghan, *Ethical Conduct: Guidelines for Government Employees* (Toronto: Institute of Public Administration of Canada, 1975), p. 13.

2. Government of Canada, *Ethical Conduct in the Public Sector: Report of the Task Force on Conflict of Interest* (Ottawa: Supply and Services, 1984), p. 29.

3. Michael Valpy, "Muzzling Employees Not in City's Interests," *Globe and Mail*, November 29, 1988, p. A8.

4. Government of Canada, *Commission of Inquiry into the Facts of Allegations of Conflict of Interest Concerning the Honourable Sinclair M. Stevens* (The Parker Commission) (Ottawa: Supply and Services, 1987), p. 25.

5. Ibid., p. 35.

6. Quoted in *John H. Spinks and Jack G. Threader* v. *Treasury Board*, Decision of the Public Service Staff Relations Board, December 22, 1986, pp. 64-65.

7. The Parker Commission, p. 30.

8. Ibid., p. 35 (emphasis added).

9. Ibid., p. 26.

10. This actual case is drawn from *Ethical Conduct in the Public Sector*, pp. 171-72.

11. The Association of the Bar of the City of New York, Special Committee on the Federal Conflict of Interest Laws, *Conflict of Interest and Federal Service* (Cambridge, Mass.: Harvard University Press, 1960), p. 6.

12. Bernard Ostry, "Ethics and Public Service," *IPAC Bulletin* 10 (December 1987), p. 3.

13. *Globe and Mail*, July 15, 1977.

14. "Behind the Boom: The Story of York Region," *Globe and Mail*, November 2, 1988.

15. See Kenneth Kernaghan, *The Alan Jeffrey Affair*, Case Program in Canadian Public Administration (Toronto: Institute of Public Administration of Canada, 1977).

16. *Gerald William McKendry and The Treasury Board (Department of Regional Economic Expansion)*, Decision of the Public Service Staff Relations Board, December 19, 1972, pp. 84-106

17. Maureen H. Taylor and Alan E. Filmer, "Moonlighting: The Practical Problems," *Canadian Public Administration* 29 (Winter 1986), p. 594.

18. Ibid., p. 595.

19. *Max Bilkoski and Treasury Board (Employment and Immigration Canada)*, Decision of the Public Service Staff Relations Board, July 24, 1987.

20. *Legault and Treasury Board (Post Office Department)*, Decision of the Public Service Staff Relations Board, December 19, 1976, pp. 31-32.

21. *Ethical Conduct in the Public Sector*, p. 22.

22. For elaboration of these techniques, see ibid., pp. 63-73.

Chapter 7

The Accountable Public Servant

Public servants have a traditional duty to account for their decisions to elected officials who in turn are accountable to the public. In the past few decades the growth in the size and power of public bureaucracies has heightened public concern about their accountability and the meaning of the traditional duty has become a matter of considerable debate. Public servants are now required to be accountable to a variety of political actors both within and outside government; as a result, they are often uncertain as to whom and for what they are accountable.[1]

This chapter is concerned with what is meant by the duty to be accountable. Does accountability mean the same thing as responsibility? Why is the accountability of public servants important? How is the duty to be accountable related to such administrative values as efficiency, effectiveness, and responsiveness? *To whom* is a public servant accountable? To whom is a public servant *primarily* accountable? To the minister? To the legislature or municipal council? To the public? To his or her conscience? *For what* is a public servant accountable? *By what means* can public servants be held accountable?

Defining the Duty

In most governments, accountability requirements for public servants are spelled out in a plethora of statutes, regulations, and policy and procedure manuals rather that in codes of ethics or codes of conduct. However, the federal government's Statement of Management Principles explains that "depending on their level and authority, there are two broad areas of accountability for managers: for *policy performance*, that is, for the provision of advice and the achievement of results in the context of government objectives; and for *administrative performance*, which includes the stewardship of public resources, adherence to the laws and to the direction provided by Cabinet and the central agencies."[2] The Ontario government has gone further by giving accountability a prominent place in its management philosophy and by explaining briefly, in a separate document, the meaning of accountability, how it fits into the management process, what managers are accountable for, and how they are held accountable.[3] Even these modest efforts are not matched by most other governments. Thus, it is essential to examine the meaning and implications of the current duty to be accountable.

The concept of accountability is closely related to that of responsibility. There is widespread agreement in the academic public administration community that the concept of administrative responsibility has two related components, namely *objective* responsibility (or accountability) and *subjective* (or personal) responsibility.[4]

Objective responsibility is very similar in meaning to the notion of accountability; it refers to the responsibility which a public servant has "to someone else, outside of self, for some thing or some kind of performance."[5] It is accompanied by sanctions for failure to carry out assigned duties. Objectively responsible behavior is that behaviour which is in accord with the formal requirements of the law and the organizational hierarchy.

Subjective responsibility, however, refers to the responsibility which a public servant feels toward individuals, groups, and organizations. It is normally associated with considerations of loyalty and conscience rather than accountability and answerability. Subjective responsibility is a more inclusive notion than objective responsibility in that a public servant can feel responsible to a much wider range of political actors than those to whom he or she is formally accountable. For example, a public servant may feel a sense of responsibility to pressure groups or to the general public even though he or she is not directly accountable to them.

H.L. Laframboise makes a similar distinction between what he terms dependent accountability and independent accountability. He explains that dependent accountability "is objective, responding to processes imposed by others, called to account by them and dependent on their judgment" whereas independent accountability "is subjective. Its base is personal integrity – the quality or state of sound moral principle – uprightness, honesty and sincerity coupled with a sense of wholeness derived from truth to one's inner self. One in effect calls one's self to account for one's actions."[6]

Despite this conceptual distinction, in practice many academics and public servants use the terms accountability and responsibility interchangeably. It is common to speak of the accountability of public servants to the public, to client groups, or to their conscience (that is, responsibility in the subjective sense) as if this were the same kind of relationship as the accountability which public servants owe to their political or administrative superiors. To avoid confusion, we will interpret accountability in this broad sense. We will, however, differentiate between *direct* and *indirect* accountability. As explained in chapter 2, in a Westminster-style government such as ours, public servants are not directly accountable to any individuals, groups or organizations outside the executive branch of government; thus, they are only indirectly accountable to such important political actors as the legislature, the public, and client groups. In the municipal sphere of government, employees are directly accountable only to elected officials and administrative superiors.

The Royal Commission on Financial Management and Accountability (the Lambert Commission) noted that "accountability, like electricity, is difficult to define" but it argued that:

> "accountability relies on a system of connecting links – a two-way circuit involving a flow of information that is relevant and timely, not only for managers but for those who must scrutinize the decisions and deeds of managers. We gauge its presence when we observe that a certain *discipline* has been imposed upon those who are assigned roles and duties in the system. In simple terms, accountability is that quality of a system that obliges the participants to *pay attention* to their respective assigned and accepted responsibilities."[7]

Thus, a useful working definition of accountability is *the obligation to answer for the fulfilment of assigned and accepted duties within the framework of the authority and resources provided.*
This brief definition requires elaboration because it does not specify *to whom* public servants are accountable. Moreover, its reference to assigned duties addresses only superficially the question of *for what* public servants are accountable and it does not cover the matter of sanctions for failure to fulfill one's duties. It does, however, make an important addition to the traditional definition of accountability which emphasized strict answerability for performance, especially for financial performance. The definition used here implies that penalties for failing to fulfill one's duties may be ameliorated in circumstances where sufficient resources and authority have not been available. It also adds the notion of *accepted* duties to suggest that the duties for which public servants are to be held accountable should be as clearly specified as possible during discussions with hierarchical superiors (see cases 7.2 and 7.3). Hence the significance for achieving accountability of such management techniques as management by objectives and performance appraisals.

The Importance of Accountability

Accountability is an enduring value not only in government but in society generally. Indeed, accountability is often treated as an ethical principle, that is, as a rule which provides a guide for ethical behaviour. Individuals have a deep personal interest in ensuring that those persons who exercise authority over them, whether they be corporate leaders, union leaders, medical professionals, or public servants, are held to account for the exercise of that authority. Those who exercise such authority are well advised to consider the importance of accountability from behind a "veil of ignorance." If they didn't know what their position in life was going to be, what measure of accountability would they deem appropriate?
Accountability takes on special importance in the context of responsible government in general and responsible public service in particular. There are good reasons in both democratic and public administration theory to hold public servants accountable. We live in a democratic political system where the legitimacy of the government is supposed to be based on the consent of the governed. Through

democratic elections, this consent is given to ministers and legislators, not to public servants. The Westminster model on which the Canadian system is based requires that the cabinet as a collectivity and the ministers individually be accountable to the legislature and through the legislature to the public. Public servants are accountable to their political superiors for implementing the policies put forward by the government and approved by a democratically elected legislature.

Nevertheless, public servants necessarily exercise a great deal of power in the development and implementation of public policy. It is now generally acknowledged that effective government requires considerable delegation of power to expert and experienced public servants. Holding public servants accountable for the exercise of this power is one of the major issues of contemporary governance, not only in Canada but around the world. The expansion in bureaucratic power that has resulted from the growth in the scale and complexity of government has made it more difficult for the public or their elected representatives to hold public servants accountable for its exercise.

An often-neglected offsetting development, however, is the increased speed of communications which makes it easier for the head offices of government departments to control and monitor the activities of their field personnel. For example, the scope and intensity of the audit function have increased because electronic data can be easily checked for coherence and consistency. A persuasive argument could be made that public servants are more accountable than ever. The nature and extent of this accountability depend to a large extent of course on the public servants' position and level in the hierarchy.

It is notable also that mechanisms for promoting administrative accountability have emerged largely in an *ad hoc*, unco-ordinated fashion to cope with the gradual expansion of bureaucratic power. Thus, the challenge is both to provide an adequate array of accountability mechanisms and to ensure that taken together these mechanisms constitute a coherent system. For example, techniques to hold public servants accountable to legislative committees for tasks for which they are already accountable to ministers create conflicting accountabilities. As explained below, the complexity of our political and administrative institutions and processes means that a system without some conflicting accountabilities is an elusive goal.

Not only is administrative accountability centrally important to democratic thought and practice; it is also integrally linked to the concept of the public interest and to the constitutional conventions of ministerial responsibility and political neutrality discussed in earlier chapters. In determining the public interest, public servants often have to reconcile conflicting accountabilities, for example, to their political superior and to their profession. Moreover, the content of a system of administrative accountability depends heavily on the extent to which the government and individual ministers wish to preserve and strengthen the responsibility of ministers and the political neutrality of public servants. For example, a system where public servants were directly and significantly accountable to legislators, especially for policy matters, would be a substantial departure from accepted constitutional conventions of parliamentary government.

The importance of accountability arises also from the fact that it has been a central and enduring value in the evolution of the theory and practice of public administration. A persuasive argument could be made that accountability has been the dominant administrative value over the past 15 years and is likely to remain so for the foreseeable future. Why has accountability become so important? In large part because of the government's need to ensure that public money is spent as efficiently and effectively as possible during a time of economic restraint. Thus accountability is closely tied to the administrative values of efficiency and effectiveness. These three values are not of course necessarily complementary. For example, implementing the directives of one's political superiors may in some cases mean implementing a program which is inefficient or ineffective, or both.

Accountability frequently clashes with other values also. A public servant's effort to be responsive in the sense of serving the public well may clash with his or her accountability to an administrative superior who has given instructions to reduce the level of service or a public servant who is appointed in part to remedy the historical underrepresentation of native people in the public service may on occasion be torn between taking action to promote their interests and being accountable to the wishes of an administrative superior. In such instances, public servants have to decide to whom accountability is owed.

Accountability to Whom?

It is easy to compile a long list of the individuals, groups, organizations, institutions, and standards to which public servants are routinely advised to be accountable. Some writers on accountability focus on entities to which public servants are directly accountable, that is, political and administrative superiors; others add entities to which public servants are only indirectly accountable, for example, legislators, the public, and client groups; still others talk about the accountability of public servants to professional standards, conscience, and the public interest.[8] Another popular approach is to divide the public servant's accountability relationships into categories such as political accountability (to ministers or legislators), legal accountability (to the courts or administrative tribunals), hierarchical accountability (to political and administrative superiors), and professional accountability (to the standards of one's profession).

Regardless of the way in which the public servant's accountability relationships are classified, it is easy to see the likelihood of conflicts between and among these relationships. Public servants are often accountable in several directions at once and can, therefore, receive conflicting signals as to what is expected of them. Herbert Kaufman has observed that "in any large organization, subordinates inevitably receive clashing and contradictory cues and signals from above ... Despite efforts to reconcile instructions, many directives come down without regard to those from other sources. When this happens, subordinates may have to decide for themselves what their situations require, picking and choosing among the directives for justification."[9] Not all public servants have the same scope of accountability relationships. Much depends on the position they hold and its location in the organizational pyramid. Clearly, a deputy minister has a much more complicated set of accountability relationships than a file clerk. But even at the middle levels of the hierarchy, public servants are accountable in a variety of directions: upward to hierarchical superiors, laterally to administrative peers, downward to administrative subordinates, outward to legislators, clients and citizens, and inward to conscience.

The lines of authority are less clearly drawn in public organizations than in business organizations. "In business, those in charge of developing and implementing policy are usually pretty well identified and the lines of authority and responsibility fairly clearly drawn. In the public sector, everybody gets into the act ... As a result the decision-making process is extremely slow and time-consuming, lines of authority are uncertain and responsibility for what emerges is ill-defined."[10] A federal public service executive has been quoted as saying that "when you are getting your advice as to what you are supposed to do, you get it from the Privy Council Office, from the Treasury Board Secretariat, from the Public Service Commission, from Cabinet and from your Minister. There is no coherence in direction. In fact, there is just more conflict and, finally, there are no criteria that you can use to make the judgment."[11]

The nature and effects of conflicting accountability requirements in the public service can be demonstrated by an actual, but not necessarily a typical, case from the federal sphere of government:

RECONCILING CONFLICTING MANDATES:
PURCHASING A PRINTING PRESS

The Surveys and Mapping Branch of the Department of Energy, Mines and Resources (EMR) had produced maps of Canada for nearly 100 years. In 1975, the Branch noted escalating operating costs due to frequent breakdown of its obsolete printing presses. The Branch requisitioned a modern printing press through the Department of Supply and Services (DSS). DSS advised that three issues needed to be resolved prior to procurement: DSS's own mandate to provide printing services seemed to conflict with the printing activity at EMR; the EMR printing work might more economically be contracted out; it might be advisable to. consolidate the DSS and EMR printing activities.

Agreement could not be reached, and both departments marshalled opinions in support of their respective views in a lengthy dispute that involved a succession of ministers and senior officials on both sides. The only point on which both parties agreed was that an additional printing capacity was required.

After nearly four years of dispute, EMR prepared a Treasury Board submission to seek approval for the acquisition. Treasury Board Secretariat concluded, however, that it was not the Treasury Board's role to arbitrate such disputes. It urged the two departments to reconcile their differences on their own.

The controversy was not resolved until January 1983, when the Minister for Mines insisted on making a submission to Treasury Board. The Board decided that EMR should get its new printing press.

The elapsed time from original requisition to final approval was seven years. During all this period, the dispute had focused mainly on the mandate question – on who had the right to print maps. According to one study, EMR could have saved over $900, 000 in operating costs, had it been able to install a new press at the time of the original requisition.[12]

In another case, four departments took almost two years to reach agreement on which department should chair an interdepartmental committee. No common review mechanism existed to resolve the dispute. To oblige the departments to reach a consensus, the cabinet had to authorize the withholding of funds that had already been approved. This case is especially significant because the committee's task was to control activities related to the use and disposal of highly toxic chemicals. It is notable also that there are 58 Acts of Parliament governing the use of toxic chemicals, and 24 federal departments and agencies are engaged in toxic-chemical-related activities.[13] It is not surprising that accountability for action (or lack of action) is sometimes blurred.

The problem of conflicting accountability requirements is closely related to that of excessive accountability requirements. One of the top ten constraints on government productivity identified by federal public service executives in a 1983 study by the auditor general was administrative regulations; these were described as "too many, too detailed and too universal." This problem persists in most public bureaucracies today despite efforts to eliminate many of these rules, to turn rules into guidelines, and to delegate authority for achieving results. A typical complaint is that "there are too many rules in various areas such as personnel, finance, and administration. You can prove they reduce costs, but the loss in terms of productivity is so much greater."[14] The strong links between conflicting and excessive accountabilities on the one hand and such administrative values as efficiency and effectiveness on the other can easily be seen.

In the Canadian context, much of the discussion of competing accountability relationships centres on the role of deputy ministers. Deputies occupy the highest posts in the public service, with the result that their accountability relationships provide a framework for the accountability of their subordinates. Moreover, in our Westminster-style government deputies perform a difficult but critically important balancing act on the tightrope between the political and bureaucratic realms of government. As noted in chapter 3, public servants, especially at the highest levels, are expected to maintain their balance by being politically sensitive but not politically partisan. Compared to all other public servants, deputies are in closer direct contact with elected officials, not only with ministers to whom they are directly accountable but also with legislators with whom they have formal, public contact in legislative committees. Given the complicated web of accountabilities in which deputies are entangled, much can be learned from their experience as to how conflicting accountabilities can be resolved at other levels of the hierarchy.

Both legislators and members of the public complain that on occasion nobody, including ministers and deputy ministers, seems to be accountable for certain government actions. For example, an opposition member of the Ontario legislature, during his questioning of the secretary of Management Board, stated:

> You say it is not up to you . . . You are not responsible. The deputy ministers are not responsible. They are not going reveal [the information] or the ministers are not going to reveal it. Walker [a Cabinet minister] says he is not going to give it because it is his previous ministry. The present minister says he is not going to reveal it because . . . it relates to a previous minister. The Premier says he is not going to reveal it because it is up to the ministers or to the auditor or to Management Board. You as Management Board say you are not going to [reveal it] because it is not your responsibility. You completely abdicated that responsibility and decentralized your authority. Who the hell is responsible, then?[15]

Concerns about gaps in the accountability of the governors to the governed have given rise to the suggestion that public servants should be held directly accountable to the legislature. This suggestion requires an answer to the question: to whom do public servants owe their primary loyalty? Do you accept the traditional view that in our Westminster-style government public servants are accountable first of all to their minister and that they are only indirectly accountable to the legislature and to the public through their minister? Or do you agree with those public servants who claim that their primary accountability is to the public? Or could you make a persuasive argument that public servants should consider themselves primarily accountable to the elected representatives of the people gathered in the legislature? The IPAC Statement of Principles answers these questions with the assertion that "public employees are accountable on a day-to-day basis to their superiors for their own actions and the actions of their subordinates. They owe their primary duty, however, to their political superiors. They are indirectly accountable to the legislature or (municipal) council and to the public through their political superiors."

It is difficult to hold public servants directly accountable to the public. What mechanisms could be devised to permit such accountability when even mechanisms by which public servants can effectively *consult* the public are so difficult to devise? (see chapter 5 on service to the public). It is more practicable and, in our political system, more legitimate to hold public servants directly accountable to the legislature. The Lambert Commission, in support of its argument that Parliament is the beginning and end of the chain of accountability in the Canadian political system, recommended the strengthening of parliamentary committees so that they could exert more effective control over the executive. The commission recognized, however, that *direct* accountability of public servants to legislative committees could reasonably be required only with respect to a limited portion of the responsibilities of a limited number of public servants. It recommended that deputy ministers be held directly accountable to the Public Accounts Committee of the House of Commons for the performance of specific delegated or assigned duties. Is this limited direct accountability of deputies to a single legislative committee a feasible means of promoting the accountability of public servants to the elected representatives of the people and, through them, to the public? We shall return to this question.

The issue of multiple accountabilities is further complicated by clashes between the accountability of public servants to the standards of their profession and accountability to their political and administrative superiors. Governments employ large numbers of persons belonging either to the general professions (law, medicine, engineering) or to the specifically public service professions (social workers, school teachers, military officers). The expertise of these professionals is essential to effective policy development and execution. Moreover, their professional standards prompt many of them to accept individual responsibility for their actions. But do these benefits justify greater freedom from hierarchical control for professionals than for other public servants? Is it appropriate for professionals, as compared to other public servants, to act more on the basis of subjective responsibility? Can professional public servants justify blowing the whistle on government wrongdoing by reference to their profession's ethical standards? Should professional public servants be required to do any

---

CASE 7.1
MIXED MESSAGES

The following conversation is overheard between Laura and Elliot, two government social workers.

Laura: I guess you did what you thought was best, Elliot. I hope you haven't made a mistake.

Elliot: It's a chance I'll have to take.

Laura: What were you thinking of?

Elliot: That woman was desperate, Laura. She had nowhere else to turn. I was afraid that if I didn't approve the emergency funds for her she would do something drastic.

Laura: But you know as well as I do that ministry policy states clearly that emergency funds are to be used only to supply clients with food, shelter, and clothing in times of crisis.

Elliot: It was a crisis. Her husband abandoned her with three small children; she has no marketable skills; and she can't work in any case because she has no one to look after the kids. When she asked me for additional funds to buy a used washer and dryer, I couldn't refuse. With three children, she was piling the kids and the laundry on the bus every day to go to the laundromat. That can be costly too.

Laura: But to disobey ministry policy...

Elliot: We're professionals, Laura, and as such we are accountable to our clients. Many of them have no one else to turn to. We can't just turn our backs on them because of some arbitrary policy the ministry adopts.

Laura: Well, Elliot, I hope for your sake that the ministry audit branch sees it that way.

ISSUES

− Do Elliot's professional responsibilities require him to act as he did?

− Can Elliot resolve the problem of conflicting accountabilities? If so, how?

---

more than bring their professional concerns, for example, about costs or safety, to the attention of the political decision-makers? Do professionals have a greater duty of accountability to their clients than other public servants do? Can they, for example, push up costs in order to meet needs that are defined on the basis of their professional knowledge and ethic?

The kind of accountability dilemma that arises for professional public servants is demonstrated well in case 7.1 where a public servant who is a professional social worker violates ministry regulations to assist a client who is considered to be especially needy. Did the social worker act responsibly in this case?

Accountability for What?

There is a close relationship between the issue of *to whom* public servants are accountable and the issue of *for what* they are accountable. Moreover, both issues are closely linked to a public servant's level and position in the administrative hierarchy.

Public servants at the lower levels of the service face a relatively simple accountability system: they are primarily accountable to their hierarchical superior for the accomplishment of fairly clearly specified tasks. They may feel a sense of accountability to other entities within or outside government, but they have little authority or influence to indulge this feeling. In general, as we move toward the middle and upper levels of the service, accountability relationships become more numerous and complex. This does not mean, however, that accountability is not important at lower levels. "As one proceeds upwards in the management hierarchy, the scope of a manager's responsibilities increases, but the requirement of accountability remains constant at all levels. The lowest manager in the hierarchy is as accountable for his actions as the most senior ministry executive."[16]

The nature and extent of accountability requirements depend also on the public servant's position, including the administrative unit or policy field in which the position is located and the extent to which it requires the exercise of professional expertise. A greater number and variety of political actors will be intensely concerned about the accountability of public servants in the policy field of unemployment insurance than in that of veterans affairs. Moreover, public servants occupying positions demanding highly professional competence will usually be subject to less stringent accountability requirements because reliance can be placed on professional standards of performance. This is the case, for example, in the area of environmental protection, where judgments about appropriate safety standards

---

CASE 7.2
WHO'S TO BLAME?

The following comments of Ada, a regional manager, are overheard after a staff meeting where she was blamed for the failure of a recent program.

Ada: (angrily) I refuse to take the blame for the failure of that program. It was a disaster right from the start. I guess I should have complained earlier. We had almost no input into the details of the mandate, and the advice of our experts on key issues was largely ignored. The policy my division was expected to implement was poorly conceived and badly designed. How do you run a program like that efficiently and effectively?

They have the gall to blame me for overspending on the program. How could I have done otherwise given the situation? I wasn't consulted about the specific targets for the fiscal year, and as if that wasn't bad enough, I wasn't given enough resources to carry out the program in any case. It was a hopeless situation. I think I did a terrific job, all things considered. There is just no way they can hold me accountable for this.

ISSUES
– Should you take on jobs you can't do?
– What would be the minimum conditions under which Ada could be held accountable?

---

sometimes have to be based on scientific evidence that does not permit confident conclusions about the degree of risk involved. In other areas, for example building inspection, where the requisite level of technical expertise may not be as high, accountability requirements may still be relatively loose because of the need for public servants to exercise considerable discretion to get the job done effectively. The degree to which accountability requirements can be applied across the public service as a whole is severely limited by such considerations. Accountability systems must be tailored not only to particular departments but also to particular units and positions within departments.

The level and position which public servants occupy in the hierarchy also determine the extent to which they are involved in policy development and policy execution. Public servants, especially at more senior levels, are accountable to a variety of entities for the quality of both their policy advice and their program implementation. For example, deputy ministers are formally accountable to several authorities for providing policy advice to ministers, for helping ministers fulfill their accountability to the legislature and the public, for contributing to the collective management of the government, and for managing their department.

The IPAC Statement of Principles notes that "public employees are accountable for the quality of their advice, for carrying out assigned duties and for achieving policy and program objectives within the framework of law, prevailing constraints, direction from their superiors, and the limits of authority and resources at their disposal." Note that this Principle not only specifies what public servants are accountable for but suggests the circumstances under which they should be held accountable. Implicit in the Principle is the notion that public servants should be held accountable only "for the fulfilment of assigned and accepted duties within the framework of the authority and resources provided." This notion of limited accountability is clear in the Ontario government's statement of the necessary conditions for the maintenance of accountability in the public service. These conditions are as follows:

- Authority and responsibility must be delegated.

- Plans, objectives and guidelines must be clearly defined.

- Adequate information and reporting systems must be in place.

- Managers must define the results that they are working to achieve. These defined results must be agreed upon by superiors and accepted by managers with responsibility for implementing the program.

- Suitable mechanisms must be in place for measuring and evaluating managerial performance.[17]

Managers must, therefore, ensure that they design and operate effectively an accountability system which fulfills these conditions. The accountability of the public servants in cases 7.2 and 7.3 can be assessed not only in terms of what they are accountable for but also more specifically in terms of the extent to which such conditions were met. We shall see, in our discussion of performance evaluation in the next section, that such conditions for accountability are not easy to fulfill.

Contemporary discussions and definitions of accountability emphasize the importance not only of defining clearly the duties for which public servants will be held accountable but also of ensuring that public servants *accept* the assigned duties. Clearly, it is not intended that public servants should be permitted to reject duties assigned by hierarchical superiors; rather it is intended that superiors and subordinates seek mutual agreement on duties to be performed and results to be achieved. Provision must be made for appeal to a higher authority when agreement cannot be reached.

We have suggested to this point that public servants are accountable to a variety of entities for the quality of their performance, subject to the availability of adequate authority and resources. There remains the question of the *means* by which these various entities can hold public servants accountable.

Accountability by What Means?

Given the several individuals, groups, and organizations to whom public servants are directly or indirectly accountable, it is not surprising that there is a wide variety of means by which public servants can be held accountable. These range from internal administrative techniques such as performance appraisals, which are used by administrative superiors, to consultative mechanisms such as advisory boards involving members of the public or client groups. It is understandable that in general public servants should be most anxious to satisfy those individuals or organizations to whom they are directly accountable, namely their hierarchical superiors and the central agencies; these are the entities with the authority and resources to bestow rewards and impose penalties. Internal administrative controls are centrally important in an accountability system. This can be seen even at the very peak of the administrative hierarchy in government where deputies are held accountable to central agencies, notably treasury or management boards, for sound management, including the effectiveness of the accountability system in their department.

It is not possible to examine here the full range of the means by which public servants can be held directly or indirectly accountable. We will, therefore, focus on two mechanisms of particular current interest. The first of these, *performance appraisal* (or performance

---

CASE 7.3
DON'T BLAME ME!

Gary, the head of planning for the federal Department of Transport is overheard after his division's advice resulted in the construction of a "white elephant" airport.

Gary: I gave you the best possible advice. We used the best techniques for analysis, and we had the best data. That advice was technically sound. That's all I can be held accountable for. I'm not accountable for policy decisions at all. The minister chose to build that airport. If the policy was a mistake, that's not my problem. I'm just responsible for giving you advice. I can't be held accountable for the fact that oil prices went up and there was a major downturn in the economy. Air travel just didn't increase at the rate we had anticipated, and airlines didn't support the idea of moving their hub operations. They can't hold me responsible for the failure of that airport!

ISSUES
– Do you support Gary's position?
– What is a planner or policy adviser accountable for?
– Were all the requirements for accountability met?

---

evaluation), is an internal mechanism that is used in part to promote accountability; the second, *direct accountability to legislative committees*, is an external mechanism that has been proposed as a means of enhancing the accountability of public servants to the elected representatives of the people.

Performance appraisal is a technique for collecting and analyzing in a systematic fashion information on the performance of employees. It involves two key elements, performance review and employee appraisal. Performance review is "a continuous process in which a supervisor and an employee consider the duties to be performed by the employee, the achievements expected, the evaluation criteria and the results actually achieved." Employee appraisal is based on performance review; it "identifies an employee's various qualifications, estimates potential, identifies and proposes responses to training and development needs, and indicates future assignments."[18] The link between performance appraisal and accountability can easily be seen by referring to the definition of accountability provided earlier. The performance review component of performance appraisal requires that an employee's duties be assigned by a superior and accepted by the employee.

While performance appraisal is a valuable technique for enhancing accountability, it is an imprecise instrument which has been characterized by a great deal of controversy. Its use gives rise to important ethical issues, in large part because there is so much room in the process for the exercise of subjective judgment. Banner and Cooke single out five specific ethical dilemmas associated with performance appraisal. These are: the use of trait-oriented or subjective evaluation criteria; problems in the writing of performance standards and measurement indicators; the use of different performance appraisal systems within the same organization; how the results of performance appraisal are used; and who determines the objective standards.[19]

A study of private sector managers in the United States showed that the most frequently cited areas of ethical concerns (about two-thirds of the total) were "(a) performance evaluation and resultant hiring, firing, promotion, and demotion decisions; (b) designing and administering personnel policies and systems, for example, disability policies, reward systems; and (c) managing relationships on the job."[20] Banner and Cooke contend that "subjective evaluations are inherently unfair; different raters can treat the same behavior or set of behaviors differently (reliability) and there is no necessary agreement on what constitutes 'good performance' (validity)."[21] In addition, performance evaluation can be manipulated by unethical managers who advance or injure the careers of particular employees for reasons unrelated to job competence, such as personal friendship or prejudice against certain groups. This consideration is especially important in the light of current efforts to achieve employment equity by selecting and advancing members of historically disadvantaged groups. If performance appraisal is to be an effective mechanism for promoting accountability, employees must be satisfied that the process is a fair one. One way of helping to ensure fairness is to hold managers accountable for their use of the performance appraisal system.

The process of performance appraisal has become less subjective as more sophisticated techniques have been developed to measure employee performance. This advance has been accompanied by increased use of "pay for performance" systems which are designed in part to promote accountability for assigned and accepted duties. Under these systems, employees are held accountable for the achievement of objectives set out in performance agreements or performance contracts which they negotiate with their superiors. So far as possible, performance agreements contain measurable objectives for all significant components of a job.

The subjective aspect of performance appraisal is, however, still evident in efforts to hold public servants accountable, even for assigned and accepted duties. We noted above that certain conditions should be met if public servants are to be held strictly accountable for their performance. These conditions place a heavy burden on managers to ensure that employees are not penalized for failing to achieve objectives which are beyond their control. Employees are expected to make a genuine effort to achieve their objectives within the framework of the resources available to them, but it is not easy to assess the extent to which achieving these objectives has been beyond the employees' control. Under these circumstances, managers are often reluctant to impose penalties for what may actually be poor performance.

The same argument can be made with regard to the accountability of public servants to political actors other than immediate superiors. For example, if public servants were held directly accountable to legislative committees,[22] they could try to justify failure to achieve certain objectives on the grounds of insufficient resources. It is likely to be more difficult for legislators than for public service managers to assess the validity of such claims.

We have already mentioned the Lambert Commission proposal that deputy ministers be held directly accountable to the Public Accounts Committee of the legislature for certain administrative duties.[23] The commission argued that this innovation would not interfere with the doctrine of ministerial responsibility; rather it "would reinforce the minister's and the Cabinet's ability to be responsible for the conduct of the affairs of government . . . by reinforcing the internal processes that give individual ministers, and the collectivity, the means of knowing whether deputy heads are carrying out their jobs effectively."[24]

Those who oppose this proposal contend that it is difficult in practice to distinguish sharply the administrative matters for which public servants would be held accountable from the policy matters for which ministers would be held accountable. We concluded in chapter 3 that politics, policy, and administration are closely intertwined. Moreover, an important component of an effective accountability system is a clear statement of the objectives being sought. Since we know that ministers often cannot provide a clear statement of policy objectives, it would be inappropriate to hold public servants accountable for "their effectiveness in achieving policy goals." It is argued also that holding public servants directly – and publicly – accountable to the Public Accounts Committee would bring them more into the public eye and thereby diminish their anonymity. Finally, there is concern that direct accountability of deputies to a legislative committee would undermine ministerial responsibility by making it more difficult for ministers to hold deputies accountable. The lines of accountability would be confused rather than clarified.[25]

This debate demonstrates the difficulty of holding public servants accountable to the legislature or to the public through the legislature. It also reinforces the significance for achieving accountability of internal administrative mechanisms such as performance appraisal. Are the best means for promoting accountability to be found in mechanisms by which public servants control one another? We have seen that mechanisms such as performance appraisal are far from perfect instruments for this purpose. Then why not have public servants control *themselves*? To what extent can we rely on their sense of personal responsibility?

Accountability and Personal Responsibility

We noted earlier that accountability is tightly linked to the values of efficiency and effectiveness; indeed, many of the mechanisms in an accountability system are designed in part to achieve the efficient and effective use of public resources. Nevertheless, the proliferation of accountability mechanisms and the heavy reporting and record-keeping duties they require often detract from the time and energy public servants can devote to developing policies and delivering programs. Gordon Osbaldeston has warned against the undue use at the most senior level of the public service of "quantitative, mechanistic standards" in such areas as financial management and personnel classification. He describes as a myth "the assumption that the only way to make sure Deputy Ministers are accountable is to establish mechanistic standards of performance or measurements for various management functions, and then [to develop] elaborate mechanisms for monitoring these functions."26 He contends that such management techniques are more appropriate for operational functions at the middle management level than at the executive level. But even at this level the many entities to which public servants are directly or indirectly accountable can be compared to the tentacles of an accountability octopus. Public servants can spend so much time warding off these tentacles that they can't keep their heads above water long enough to do their jobs efficiently and effectively.

In recent years central agencies in many government jurisdictions have tried to reduce the paperwork burden which has resulted from the heavy emphasis on accountability. They emphasize the extent to which discretion in the management of human and financial resources has been delegated to departments and how regulations have either been abolished or replaced by guidelines. There is increasing recognition that careful consideration needs to be given not only to loosening the tentacles of the octopus but also to cutting some of them off.

Still, many public servants perceive the agencies' demands for information and for adherence to certain rules and regulations as unnecessarily constraining. In such circumstances, is it ethical for public servants to deviate from established procedures? Donald Warwick responds by arguing for the ethical principle of "procedural respect." He contends that:

> established procedures are perhaps the single most important source of accountability in the public bureaucracy ... What we can ask of the public servant is not reflexive compliance with every jot and tittle of the rulebook, but a fundamental respect for established procedure ... At times the procedures may have to be circumvented in the public interest and at other times they may have to be changed. But respect demands that such actions be the exception rather than the rule, and a last rather than a first resort.27

Guidance as to what deviations from established procedure are appropriate can be found in the deontological ethical theory explained in chapter 1. Warwick restates Kant's Categorical Imperative as follows: "Seek exceptions to established procedures only when you would grant the same right to others in comparable circumstances

. . . Proponents of a deviation would have to demonstrate that their claims supersede those of others, and to accept that these others should, if they have equivalent claims, also be exempt."[28]   Consider case 7.1 in light of this argument.

It is notable that a proliferation of accountability mechanisms can lead public servants to place undue emphasis on the process as opposed to the content of public policy. A senior federal public servant has argued that the virtues of regulations are supposed to be:

> that they prevent waste and duplication. Yet, whatever they prevent may be outweighed by what they cost. There is the cost of making rules and the cost of administering them. There is also the cost of the resulting bureaucratic actions that are sometimes unresponsive and inflexible and even absurd. But the only things we ever hear about are the alleged benefits of constraints.[29]

The emphasis on process can have an adverse impact on the ability and motivation of public servants to be responsive to the needs and desires of the public they serve. Especially during a period of economic restraint in government, when accountability is viewed largely as the efficient use of scarce resources, it is understandable that responsiveness will take a back seat to the driving force of accountability. However, responsiveness may still be assigned a high rank in the value priorities of public servants who feel a keen sense of subjective or personal responsibility to particular segments of the public.

At the beginning of this chapter we distinguished between this notion of personal responsibility and that of objective responsibility which is very similar in meaning to accountability. A sense of personal responsibility is an essential component of a comprehensive and workable system of bureaucratic responsibility; thus, formal measures to promote accountability must be complemented by efforts to stimulate a sense of personal responsibility.

The notion of personal responsibility can both complement and clash with accountability. For example, if a public servant's sense of personal responsibility is in tune with the minister's instruction to assist a disadvantaged minority group, the instruction is likely to be implemented well. In this situation, application of both the utilitarian and deontological ethical theories outlined in chapter 1 may lead the public servant to the same conclusion about the appropriate course of action. On other occasions, however, "subordinates may know precisely what is expected of them, be perfectly capable of doing it, and still not do it. What they are asked to do may offend their personal principles or their interpretation of professional ethics or their extra-organizational loyalties and commitments or their self interest ... When orders from above conflict sharply with their values, they quietly construe the orders in a way that makes them tolerable."[30] Is such behaviour responsible?

Public servants are encouraged to be creative in resolving a clash between their duty of accountability to hierarchical superiors and their sense of personal responsibility to such entities as the public or their profession. Terry Cooper uses the term moral imagination to refer to "the requisite skill for meshing the two [senses of responsibility] without a loss of integrity."[31] If the conflict of accountabilities endures, public servants are normally expected to adhere to formal accountability requirements. However, as explained in the preamble to the IPAC Statement of Principles, "public employees experience conflicts of values or loyalties" and "on occasion difficult decisions facing public employees can ultimately be resolved only by resorting to individual conscience." While for some decisions conscience may be the court of last resort, for most decisions public servants should have a clear idea of to whom and for what they are accountable and what the mechanisms are for achieving this accountability. Otherwise, how can responsible public servants fulfill their duty to be accountable?

Notes

1. John W. Langford, "Responsibility in the Public Service: Marching to Different Drummers," *Canadian Public Administration*, vol. 27 (Winter 1984), p. 521.

2. Treasury Board of Canada, *Principles for the Management of the Public Service of Canada* (Ottawa: Supply and Services, 1983), p. 9.

3. Ontario, Management Board of Cabinet, *Accountability*, OPS Management Series, Overview 5-2 (Ontario: Queen's Printer, 1982).

4. Frederick C. Mosher, *Democracy in the Public Service* (New York: Oxford University Press, 1968), pp. 7-10. See also Kenneth Kernaghan, "Responsible Public Bureaucracy: A Rationale and a Framework for Analysis," *Canadian Public Administration* 16

(Winter 1973), pp. 572-603, and Terry L. Cooper, *The Responsible Administrator* (Port Washington, N.Y.: Kennikat Press, 1982), ch. 2.

5.   Mosher, *Democracy in the Public Service*, p. 7.

6.   H.L. Laframboise, "Conscience and Conformity: The Uncomfortable Bedfellows of Accountability," *Canadian Public Administration* 26 (Fall 1983), p. 326.

7.   Royal Commission on Financial Management and Accountability, *Final Report* (Ottawa: Supply and Services, 1979), pp. 9-10 (emphasis in original).

8.   The Lambert Commission listed 10 possible sources of responsibility for federal deputy ministers: the public, Parliament, the prime minister, cabinet, the Privy Council Office, Treasury Board, Treasury Board Secretariat, the Public Service Commission, the Committee of Senior Officials, and themselves (personally); see *Final Report*, p. 490.

9.   Herbert Kaufman, *Administrative Feedback* (Washington, D.C.: Brookings Institution, 1973), p. 2.

10.   Grant Reuber, "Better Bureaucracies," *Policy Options* 3 (September-October 1982), p. 11.

11.   Office of the Auditor General, *Report* (Ottawa: Supply and Services, 1983), p. 69.

12.   Ibid., p. 67.

13.   Ibid., p. 63.

14.   Ibid., p. 69.

15.   Ontario, *Standing Committee on Public Accounts*, December 1, 1983 (typescript of proceedings).

16.   Ontario, Management Board of Cabinet, *Accountability*, p. 3.

17.   Ibid., p. 4.

18.   Government of Canada, Treasury Board Secretariat, *Personnel: A Manager's Handbook* (Ottawa: Supply and Services, 1982), p. 49.

19.   David K. Banner and Robert Allan Cooke, "Ethical Dilemmas in Performance Appraisal," *Journal of Business Ethics* 3 (1984), pp. 331-32.

20. Barbara Ley Toffler, *Tough Choices: Managers Talk Ethics* (New York: John Wiley, 1986), p. 13.

21. Banner and Cooke, p. 331.

22. For an examination of contemporary relations between public servants and federal legislators, see S.L. Sutherland and Y. Baltacioglu, *Parliamentary Reform and the Federal Public Service* (London: National Centre for Management Research and Development, University of Western Ontario, 1988).

23. For an examination of this issue, see Robert D. Carman, "Accountability of Senior Public Servants to Parliament and its Committees," *Canadian Public Administration* 27 (Winter 1984), pp. 550-55. For a comprehensive treatment of the accountability of deputy ministers, see Gordon F. Osbaldeston, *Keeping Deputy Ministers Accountable* (Toronto: McGraw Hill-Ryerson, 1989).

24. *Final Report*, p. 375.

25. Note, however, that in British departments a senior official known as an "accounting officer" answers directly to the Public Accounts Committee for the expenditure of public funds. This longstanding arrangement is not considered a threat to the convention of ministerial responsibility.

26. Gordon Osbaldeston, *The Myth of the Mandarin: The Role of a Deputy Minister in the Parliamentary-Cabinet System of Government* (London: National Centre for Management Research and Development, School of Business Administration, University of Western Ontario, December 1987), pp. 12-13.

27. Donald P. Warwick, "The Ethics of Administrative Discretion," in Joel Fleishman et al., eds., *Public Duties: The Moral Obligations of Public Officials* (Cambridge, Mass.: Harvard University Press, 1981), pp. 121-22.

28. Ibid., p. 122.

29. Office of the Auditor General, *Report*, 1983, p. 83.

30. Kaufman, *Administrative Feedback*, pp. 3-4.

31. Cooper, *The Responsible Administrator*, p. 54. See also pp. 23 ff.

Chapter 8

Preserving and Promoting Responsible Behaviour

In the preceding chapters we have examined the most common rules governing the behaviour of public servants. We have analyzed rules concerning the public interest, political neutrality, confidentiality, the protection of privacy, service to the public, conflict of interest and, finally, accountability. Overall, we have found that there is confusion among governments, public servants, and ethics "experts" about the meaning of these rules, the legitimacy of traditional interpretations, and how to prioritize rules and values when they clash in complex ethical dilemmas.

But even if we could achieve clarity and agreement within one government or public sector organization on what the rules should be, we would still be faced with the the challenge of making those rules work. How do we encourage individual public servants to act responsibly? How do we create a hospitable climate for responsible behaviour within public sector organizations? And how should we go about enforcing the rules and sanctioning offenders? In these tasks, we are faced with significant policy choices. Do we have to write the rules down? Should we adopt a code of conduct? What kind of a code? Is legislation necessary? Are education and training more important than sanctions? How significant are role models and leadership? Do we need an ethics commissioner or counsellor? Are criminal sanctions likely to be effective deterrents? In short, what regime should we use to regulate the behaviour of public servants and strengthen and encourage responsible public service?

The Traditional Approach

Until very recently, the approach to the enhancement of responsible public service employed by most Canadian governments has been to create new policies, rules and, occasionally, laws in response to widely visible instances of irresponsible behaviour and then to enforce them in a desultory manner until the onset of the next crisis. This stop-and-go attitude toward the management of public service ethics has resulted in a wide variety of patchwork regulations at all levels of government in Canada.

This is not to suggest that there are no commonalities. All Canadian governments can call on the anti-corruption sections of the Criminal Code to deal with the bribery of public officials, fraud, breach of trust, the sale or purchase of office and influence peddling.[1] Similarly, virtually all governments have an oath of office establishing secrecy obligations, and can use the provisions of the Official Secrets Act to try to ensure confidentiality. But after that, the various regimes diverge in a multitude of directions. A number of provinces have laid down stiff and detailed rules for municipal administrators in municipal acts. Some have further rules concerning particular issues (such as freedom of information, the protection of privacy, the pursuit of efficiency and effectiveness, political participation, public comment and conflict of interest) embedded in legislation. Some of these legally established rules of conduct are accompanied by enforcement or oversight agencies (e.g., an ombudsman, information commissioner, auditor general, or public service commission) which also double as participants in the reporting systems which many governments have established to ensure public service accountability.

Rather than resort to legislation, most Canadian governments have been inclined to write down rules for responsible administrative behaviour in the form of guidelines, directives in policy manuals, or codes of conduct. As a result of the tendency to make rules in reaction to problems, it is unusual to find all the rules governing the major value dilemmas in one place. Rules may be found in letters from the prime minister, premier, or city manager to senior officials; they may be found in minutes or bulletins from Treasury Board, the Public Service Commission, or the government-wide purchasing agency; and they may appear at the departmental or branch level, in the form of directives from senior managers to more junior employees. Even codes of conduct, which would appear to be tailor-made for one agency or a whole government to gather together its key rules, more often than not focus on a single issue – usually conflict of interest – leaving the rest of the rules in relative obscurity. When you add to this hodge-podge of written rules the large number of behavioural norms that remain at the level of unwritten conventions, you end up with almost a perfect formula for employee confusion, disinterest, and cynicism.

But the bad news about the traditional approach does not stop there. Not only are the rules ill-defined, dispersed, and inaccessible; they are also generally unenforced and often unenforceable. In many jurisdictions senior managers turn a blind eye to conflict of interest violations, inappropriate political activity, and unwarranted intrusions into the personal privacy of citizens because the effort involved in pursuing them is too great. When they do pursue them, the criminal charges or internal disciplinary actions are often thwarted by the burden of proof required and the procedural inadequacies inherent in organizations in which the rules are obscure and rarely properly administered. Finally, measures taken to discipline proven offenders have done little to enhance the traditional approach. Criminal sanctions (i.e., jail terms or fines) are extremely rare, and internal sanctions generally tend toward the lenient end of the scale (e.g., letters of reprimand as opposed to demotions, suspensions, or dismissals).

In the end, probably the most serious problem confronting the traditional method of managing unethical behaviour is the attitude of senior managers themselves. They too often take a paternalistic approach toward employees in ethical matters, dictating legalistically worded codes of conduct or new rules from on high without even a semblance of consultation. Once the rules are in place (and the crisis has ostensibly abated), they lose interest in them, doing little to foster their acceptance within the organization. This lack of leadership inevitably engenders the widespread belief that success and survival are far more important to senior management than any of the values found in the new rules or code. As a result, individual employees do not see responsible behaviour as a key component of the organizational culture and are often only too willing to cut ethical corners and ignore the rules to get things done.

Making the Rules Live

What can an organization that genuinely wants to build certain ethical values into its administrative culture do to ensure a reasonable chance of success? In the discussion which follows, we will concentrate on three key factors:

- the usefulness of a code of conduct;
- creating a hospitable institutional environment; and
- appropriate regimes of enforcement and sanctions.

We will be ignoring facile approaches or quick fixes that, in our view, offer little hope for genuine reform. We do not, for instance, attach much significance to the notion that the best way to cure the ethical abuses of the modern administrative state is to reduce its authority by diminishing its size or returning much of its discretionary power to the political executive. Despite efforts to diminish and "recapture" bureaucratic power, every indicator suggests that it will remain a very significant feature of post-industrial society. In any case, what grounds are there for assuming that lodging a greater portion of that discretionary authority in the hands of politicians will enhance the ethical dimension of public decision-making?

Nor do we believe that any one "miracle" compliance instrument (e.g., full public disclosure of all relevant assets and business activities as an antidote to conflict of interest) is likely on its own to have a significant impact on the behaviour of public servants. While some individual measures may be more effective than others, building a more responsible public service is clearly a complicated challenge involving a multi-dimensional solution.

Start With a Code of Conduct

Many commentators have raised questions about the usefulness of codes of conduct. One of the most prominent concerns, which we have already noted, is that a code too often takes the form of an incomprehensible document, constructed in isolation from those to whom it will apply. An example of this artificial kind of code is the federal government's Conflict of Interest and Post-Employment Code for Public Office Holders, which was released in 1985. It runs to 32 pages in length and is set up in 74 sections like a piece of legislation. Even the user-friendly brochure version of the code produced for public servants has 50 sections and 22 pages. Such a complicated vehicle is almost guaranteed to alienate those to whom it is supposed to apply, especially when it is handed down from above without consultation, like the Commandments.

Another disturbing feature of this code is its heavy negative tone. A traditional argument against ethical codes is that they are usually fixated by things that public servants should not do, paying virtually no attention to the positive values and behaviours that the organization is trying to foster. Many public servants find an exclusively "don't do this, don't do that" approach offensive.

Codes that are succinct, simply written, and positive also receive their share of criticism. It is argued that they tend to be too general, and therefore too vague to be helpful in the resolution of value dilemmas. This problem can be compounded when a code is expected to act as a reference point for public servants from across a wide range of government departments and agencies. It also creates difficulties in those situations in which the code is to be used for disciplinary purposes. Susan Wakefield sums up the concerns of a number of commentators when she points out that "the roles of public servants are too diverse and varied to allow one code applicable to all to serve any purpose."[2]

The central point which can be made in favour of a code of conduct for public servants is that it rescues the key values of the organization from the confusion and obscurity of unwritten convention and unread policy manuals and displays them prominently for public servants and the public to see. In a sense, a written code is the obvious antidote to the failure of traditional regimes to provide an acceptable starting point from which to launch a comprehensive offensive against unethical behaviour in the public service. It represents an opportunity to establish a consensus within the organization concerning both values to be pursued and behaviours to be avoided. It becomes a viable vehicle for communicating these values and unacceptable practices to both employees and the public. A good code can be used not only for communication and education; it can also become the focal point for consultation among colleagues and superiors about difficult ethical issues which arise in the work place. Finally, it provides the public and the public employee with an accessible and comprehensible standard against which the latter's behaviour can be judged and, if necessary, appropriate disciplinary measures determined.[3]

What Does a Good Code Look Like?

Some powerful arguments can be mustered for building a system for the enhancement and control of administrative behaviour around a good code of conduct. But what does such a code look like? On the heels of the concerns expressed about paternalism, one of the most important qualities of a good code is that it emerge from the group to which it is going to apply. This is not to suggest that a successful code must totally reflect the values of employees, and that therefore there is no room for leadership in its construction. What it does suggest is that any significant departure from prevailing group norms must be discussed with the affected employees and carefully justified.[4] Why should employees pay more than lip service to a rule the employer tries to impose on them without adequate explanation? In its 1985 code the federal government instituted, without prior or even *post facto* con-sultation, stiff new rules governing the post-employment practices of senior public servants. The result was that the rules did not "take." Many public servants did not believe that they were reasonable and had few qualms about attempting to subvert or get round them.

If a code is to have a fighting chance of becoming a living part of an organizational culture it must also be realistic. While it is counter-productive for a code to dwell exclusively on the negative, it is equally dangerous to its credibility to lumber it with lofty and undefinable principles. Codes which exhort the employee to seek sainthood if not martyrdom in the name of public service will soon be gathering dust.

By the same token, a good code is written in plain, non-legal language. Obviously, this precludes the possibility of making the code itself a piece of legislation. That, however, is no loss as rules of ethical conduct for public servants framed up as legislation have not enjoyed great success. Legislated codes, while they may have a higher public profile, lack flexibility, are hard to amend, do not make attractive socialization tools because of their stilted and negative language, and have proved difficult to enforce. They also can generate morale problems: "The machinery required for more effective administration

statements in the code is made clearer; such codes become excellent teaching tools; and they are more flexible because the commentaries can be revised and the cases updated.

This two-part approach to a code of conduct also helps to get around the concern that a comprehensive code designed to apply to the whole government is likely to be too general to deal with the narrower needs of a particular department or agency. While creating more specific, supplementary codes for individual agencies with special needs is still a viable option, it is also possible to make the general code more relevant to such circumstances by tailoring the commentaries to fit the kinds of ethical dilemmas faced by particular agencies.[7]

Making a Code Part of Day-to-Day Management

Gerald Caiden puts it bluntly: "No codifiers of ethics have ever claimed that codification alone would solve anything."[8] The best code in the world won't make any impact on the ethical tone of a public service if it is rooted in a hostile or indifferent organizational environment. Taking a more positive outlook, there are a number of steps that can be taken to make public sector organizations a hospitable setting for ethical codes and, more importantly, for the responsible public servant.

Probably the most significant prerequisite of success is the clear and continuing commitment of the senior management to the values and rules expressed in the code. As we noted earlier, employee cynicism about ethical behaviour flows most directly from the perception that senior managers are paying only lip service to "good" conduct, when what they really want is "successful" conduct, and ethics be damned. To reverse this perception, senior managers have to demonstrate early and often their determination to see the organization pursue its goals within the behavioural boundaries laid down by the code. "Each manager must know that everyone of his/her colleagues in the hierarchy has been required to adhere to the same standards as he/she must. With the leadership of the highest echelons of management, this will bring about a climate of integrity and ethical practice that all personnel will support."[9]

The key to the success of this demonstration effect is to get senior managers to act as ethical role models. The evidence suggests that employees draw their inspiration from the behaviour they see, not the speeches they hear.[10] They have to sense a consistency of behaviour that starts at the top of the organization and is reflected not only in the formal communications of their superiors, but also in the "back channel" or informal information that flows through the organization. They will not place much premium on service, fairness, accountability, political neutrality, or any other value featured in a code of conduct if they see their superiors abandoning these values in difficult circumstances. One of the singular afflictions of governmental organizations, of course, is the limited control which senior public servants have over the ethical demonstration effect of ministers. It is hard to persuade employees to avoid waste or conflicts of interest if the minister is spending public funds without regard for agreed-upon objectives or has a hand deep in the cookie jar.

Many commentators argue that leadership and role models must be supplemented by more specific efforts to ensure that employees understand the rules and values contained in the code of conduct. This means simply that the traditional practice of announcing a new code and then ignoring its existence must be abandoned in favour of a comprehensive and continuing program of ethical training or sensitization for affected employees. What is eerily absent from government organizations that claim to be concerned about responsible administrative behaviour is any habit of ethical discourse among employees. Until recently ethical issues never even appeared on the agenda of management courses. Even where they now do, the tendency is to squeeze them into a couple of hours at the end of a course, to give everyone a warm philosophical feeling and send them home "thinking." In most jurisdictions, case study material is virtually non-existent. The clear message to employees is that the ethical culture of the organization ("how we do things around here") is not nearly as important as financial or personnel management.

There is no point in having a code of conduct if no one in the organization has ever heard of it. But raising the profile of the ethical dimension of administration is not very difficult. A good way to start is to provide new employees with a thorough orientation to the values and rules contained in the code. In effect, an understanding and acknowledgment of the way the organization does business can be made a condition of employment. The process of reviewing and renewing the code can be incorporated into the normal pattern of employee training and management development. Case study material can be developed from problems which have emerged inside the organization. Employees can, where appropriate, be given specialized training designed to reinforce specific values contained in the code (e.g., responsiveness and empathy toward clients).[11] In the end, the important point is not how an organization goes about heightening employee awareness of its values and the ethical dilemmas that it commonly faces. What is important is that the organization recognize its responsibility for ongoing ethical sensitization. Without it, a code of conduct will make little impact on the behaviour of employees.

Some of the steps that can be taken to insinuate the rules and values contained in a code of conduct into the bureaucratic culture focus more on institutional reform than executive leadership or employee training. The thrust of the institutional approach is that the way the organization is set up and operates represents the most significant barrier to the enhancement of ethical public administration. It is argued, for instance, that value considerations will become more prominent features of decision-making only if individuals or small groups are made responsible for more widely defined tasks. In support of making bureaucratic work more holistic, it is also claimed that organizing work in this way also enhances productivity.[12] Proposals such as this are often attached to calls for the decentralization of decision-making within the organization as a means of confronting more employees with the significance and complexity of the value choices faced by the organization.

It is also argued that performance evaluation and incentive systems should be redesigned so that they acknowledge and reward behaviour which is line with key values in the code of conduct, even where such behaviour may cause problems for the organization in the short run.[13] Inspectors general within federal government agencies in the United States, for instance, are authorized to award $10,000 or 1 per cent of the cost saving to employees who disclose waste or fraud. In a more negative variation on this theme, the Office of Special Counsel was set up in Washington in 1978 to protect from retaliation public servants who disclosed evidence of waste, mismanagement, violations of law or regulations, or dangers to public health and safety.[14] By contrast, a motion in the House of Commons by a government backbencher urging the introduction of a bill shielding federal public servants from punishment for reporting similar wrongdoings was easily talked out.[15]

In order to encourage openness in administration, many jurisdictions in the United States have passed "sunshine laws," allowing for substantial public access to bureaucratic processes, most specifically meetings and the records of meetings. In fact, public participation in an infinite variety of guises is the most widely prescribed institutional means of enhancing ethical behaviour. Beyond the more obvious approaches (e.g., public hearings, citizens' advisory boards), Terry Cooper notes the availability of iterative techniques such as Delphi, structured group interaction and workshops. He insists that "acquaintance with these participation tools, and either the skills to employ them or access to persons with those skills, is essential for responsible public administration."16

The attachment of an ethics counsellor to an organization is among the more recent recommendations designed to encourage adherence by employees to a code of conduct. This is a provocative innovation with private sector precedents. Instead of having an administrator's or police officer's role, an ethics counsellor would be mandated only to advise public servants faced with difficult value dilemmas. He or she would help the troubled public servant to relate the rules and spirit of the code of conduct to the problem at hand, the pressures of peers and superiors, and the dictates of personal conscience. When asked, the ethics counsellor could act as a mediator between the public servant and the "system," providing at least an interim alternative to whistle-blowing, resignation, or uncomfortable acquiescence and silence. Obviously, only a highly respected senior manager somewhat detached from the hierarchical loyalties and day-to-day operations of the organization could fill such a role successfully.

Enforcement and Sanctions

While much can be done by way of role modelling, training, and institutional tinkering to encourage adherence to a code of conduct, there is no escaping the fact that the behaviour of some employees will remain unaffected by such efforts. It is, therefore, essential for governments to have in place effective processes for preventing violations of the rules and investigating, charging, and punishing those public servants who break the rules. There is, however, a great deal of controversy about how an effective system of enforcement and sanctions should be structured.

One major issue is where to place the responsibility for enforcement. The notion of establishing a separate government-wide agency to administer the code and ensure compliance with its provisions has gathered considerable momentum in recent years. The traditional approach of allowing senior management to administer ethical standards internally – subject, usually, to appeal to some form of staff relations board and, eventually, the courts – has fallen into disrepute. The level of enforcement can vary too much from agency to agency, procedural rights are too easily violated, those doing the enforcing are often too close to the actions being questioned, and the whole process is usually too complicated for most employees to understand. The half-way reform of giving responsibility for enforcement of the rules to a central agency (e.g., Treasury Board, Management Board, or Public Service Commission) may do little to ease the above concerns or to raise public confidence that the hen house is still not in the control of the fox. An increasingly popular alternative, therefore, is to entrust the enforcement of the code of conduct to a separate ethics office, commission, or board.

Although such offices exist in the United States, no Canadian government has as yet embraced the notion of a "one stop" ethics administration for public servants. The most detailed argument in favour of this model was made by the 1984 federal Task Force on Conflict of Interest. In its report it called on the government to establish an Office of Public Sector Ethics to administer the enforcement regime that the Task Force was recommending be established. The Office would have the power to:

- manage the proposed reporting and trust arrangements;
- investigate allegations that the code had been infringed;
- establish policy in certain areas (e.g., post-employment practices, political activity) and allow exceptions to the rules where appropriate;
- advise senior officials on rules and procedures relevant to problems which they were confronting; and
- educate public office-holders about the code of conduct and enforcement procedures.[17]

It is hard to find persuasive opposition to the idea of a separate government-wide agency for the enforcement of a code of conduct. The concerns which have been raised focus on the Big Brother connotations of a centralized enforcement bureaucracy and the impact which such an office would have on the effectiveness of ethical leadership by management at the agency level. There have, however, been questions raised about the precise powers that should be granted to an ethics office. Can it work without independent investigative authority? Should it have the power to apply sanctions, or should it merely pass on its findings to the superiors of those under investigation? Can the scope of its authority be reconciled with the powers of the existing scrutiny and oversight officers (e.g., the auditor general, public service commission, ombudsman, information and privacy commissioners)? While such questions require answers when designing a specific separate agency, they hardly add up to a powerful argument in favour of the status quo.

There is far more controversy about the type of enforcement procedures and sanctions that should be adopted to support a code of conduct. As we noted at the outset, the traditional techniques for keeping ethical order have come in for a lot of criticism. Oaths of office don't appear to be taken seriously any more. With a more liberal attitude toward moonlighting, it becomes less acceptable to "cleanse" public servants of conflict of interest temptations by insisting that they resign from all outside posts and divest themselves of potentially conflictual assets, or place them in some form of trust. In any case, most trust arrangements have been found technically wanting: as one wag put it, "every blind trust seems to have a seeing eye dog." As we have seen, elaborate accountability mechanisms do not guarantee accountability. And the presence of external "guardians" has not eradicated violations of the rules they are there to police. Part of the problem may be that the traditional guardians have little real power. Their investigations can be short-circuited and they are reduced to filing reports on wasteful or unfair behaviour and violations of privacy or information access rights. Where clout does exist (e.g., in relevant sections of the Criminal Code, Official Secrets Act, and Income Tax Act), it has proved difficult to use for procedural reasons. Moreover, criminal sanctions are viewed by many as overkill in conflict of interest and breach of confidentiality situations. Even job-related sanctions (suspension, dismissal, etc.) seem to have been ineffective. Finally, enforcement and sanctions seem largely irrelevant to the failure to perform duties such as protecting the public interest.

What reforms have been proposed to correct the failure of traditional enforcement techniques and sanctions? At the front end of

---

CASE 8.2
LET THE PUBLIC HAVE A CLOSER LOOK

The following conversation takes place between Lorne and Sandy, two middle managers in a provincial public service.

Lorne: I don't think codes or legal actions are worth a damn. The only way I can see of improving the ethical behaviour of public servants is more publicity. Why not just leave the problem up to auditing mechanisms? Publish any evidence of wrongdoing dug up by the auditor general, the ombudsman or the information commissioner, etc. Maybe we could even have a specialized ethics commissioner. If public servants know that their actions are being scrutinized and brought to the attention of the public, they'll be more careful.

Sandy: Is that fair? You're not giving them any guidelines to work from, but then you're saying if they misbehave they will be held up to public ridicule.

Lorne: It should be obvious to public servants how they should behave in most circumstances. The basic rule is simple – don't do anything you'd be ashamed to explain to randomly chosen members of the public. The various auditors simply become proxies for the public. Ethical behaviour wouldn't be a problem if the auditors had the power required to investigate the action of public servants and the publicity vehicles necessary to bring questionable behaviour to the attention of the public.

ISSUES
– Would increased scrutiny and publicity ensure responsible administrative behaviour, as Lorne suggests?
– Would a specialized ethics commissioner add an effective capacity for scrutiny to the existing auditing mechanisms?

---

the enforcement cycle, disclosure – and more particularly, public disclosure – of all relevant assets and potentially conflictual outside activities has been put forward as an alternative to traditional anti-conflict of interest mechanisms such as divestment, withdrawal, and trusts. The theory is that if public officials' assets and outside activities are an open book, then they will be reluctant to involve themselves in decisions that might give rise to charges of conflict of interest. If charges do arise, demonstrating guilt or innocence should be relatively straightforward. Two of the recent inquiries into conflict of interest violations have come down squarely in favour of full public disclosure.[18] As Justice Parker put it:

> If modern conflict of interest codes are to ensure that public confidence and trust in the integrity, objectivity, and impartiality of government are conserved and enhanced, they must be premised on a philosophy of public disclosure.[19]

Full public disclosure presents certain problems when applied to public servants. First, there is the sheer enormity of the numbers and the difficulties associated with managing the data base, keeping it current, and making it available to the public. Secondly, there are privacy concerns implicit in any scheme to make personal financial data available to the public and, therefore, the media. Finally, there is the matter of effectiveness. Knowing all about the outside activities and personal assets of public servants will not help to combat conflict of interest if confidentiality and anonymity combine to keep hidden the exact nature of their official duties.

The other major reform initiative focuses both on the front and back ends of the enforcement cycle. Drawing on trends in the United States, the proposal is that hefty criminal sentences be applied to those public servants caught breaking the rules. Furthermore, the existence of these stiff sanctions would be the foundation of a substantial and continuing campaign designed to scare public servants into being good. From a Canadian perspective, two years in jail and fines as high as $100,000 look like powerful medicine. But would they be any more effective than the existing, underemployed criminal sanctions?

There is no easy answer to the questions that have been raised about effective enforcement procedures and sanctions. One approach may be to give up the search for "miracle" cures and concentrate first on locating the authority to employ traditional remedies in one special purpose ethics office. The shadow cast by an ethics office dedicated exclusively to publicizing, administering, and enforcing a realistic and comprehensive code of conduct might do a great deal to reduce the incidence of violations. Enforcement procedures and sanctions, while they are important, are only one part of a complex mix of tools to encourage ethical behaviour.

CASE 8.3
PUT THEM IN THE SLAMMER

Kate and Tom, two federal public servants, are talking after a staff meeting at which a serious conflict of interest case was on the agenda.

Kate: I don't think I like the idea of using jail terms and fines to ensure ethical conduct.

Tom: You've got to force people to behave.

Kate: It seems to me to be awfully severe punishment. Take the example of a public official who accepts a bottle of liquor from one of his clients at Christmas. Turning something like this into a crime is like swatting a fly with a sledgehammer.

Tom: Yes, but maybe that official would never had accepted the bottle in the first place if he had known he might face the prospect of a court case and criminal charges. As it stands, suspensions and even job loss don't represent sufficient discouragement. Sanctions like this just don't seem to stop people from acting irresponsibly.

Kate: Maybe so, but I think jail terms and fines are a bit much. I know I would certainly be hesitant to come forward and accuse one of my employees if I knew he or she might go to jail or face a major fine.

ISSUES

– Are criminal sanctions appropriate antidotes to unethical behaviour?

– Would they be more effective than the prospect of suspension or job loss?

– Would managers be more reluctant to take on cases of unethical conduct if criminal sanctions were involved?

– Would the existence of stronger sanctions encourage public confidence and trust in the public sector?

Conclusion

In this final chapter we have focused on the problem of designing a regime of institutions, devices, procedures, and sanctions that will develop and sustain responsible administrative behaviour among public servants. We have argued for the development of realistic and accessible codes of conduct. In the absence of evidence that rules alone can be successful in promoting ethical behaviour, we have also emphasized the need to pay a lot more attention to education and role models. We have stressed the importance of moving away from "top down" systems of rules, sanctions, and scrutiny in favour of more participative and supportive mechanisms. Involving employees in discussions about the code of conduct will make them part of the rule-making process and supporters of an ethical administrative culture. Instead of constructing more elaborate enforcement and control mechanisms, we recommend instruments such as ethics counsellors to promote agency-level discussion and resolution of value conflicts. Employees must know that they can make ethical mistakes and survive. There is still a place for fair enforcement and reasonable sanctions, but good role models, training, counselling, and "bottom up" development of a code of conduct are, in our view, far more significant building blocks of a responsible public service.

Notes

1. See the Criminal Code, R.S.C. 1970, c. C-34, ss. 108-14.

2. Susan Wakefield, "Ethics and the Public Service," *Public Administration Review* 36 (November/December 1976), p. 663.

3. These and other arguments for and against codes of ethics can be found in: Kenneth Kernaghan, "Codes of Ethics and Administrative Responsibility," *Canadian Public Administration* 17 (Winter 1974), pp. 527-41; Kenneth Kernaghan, "Codes of Ethics and Public Administration: Progress, Problems and Prospects," *Public Administration* 58 (Summer 1980), pp. 207-24; Phillip Monypenny, "A Code of Ethics as a Means of Controlling Administrative Behaviour," *Public Administration Review* 13 (Summer 1953), pp. 184-87; Ralph Clark Chandler, "The Problem of Moral Reasoning in Public Administration," *Public Administration Review* 43 (January/February 1983), pp. 32-39.

4. Some authorities go further in the quest for legitimization, insisting that the public be involved in the formation of public service codes. See, for instance, Terry L. Cooper, *The Responsible Administrator* (Port Washington, N.Y.: Kennikat Press, 1982), p. 109.

5. Ibid., p. 108.

6. Kenneth Kernaghan, *Ethical Conduct: Guidelines For Government Employees* (Toronto: Institute of Public Administration of Canada, 1975), p. 11.

7. While not designed for a specific government, the Statement of Principles of the Institute of Public Administration of Canada avoided several of the deficiencies commonly associated with the development, content, and administration of codes of conduct. It was developed over a two-year period on the basis of extensive consultation with all of the Institute's members. The process of reaching a consensus on the Statement's content was considered to be an extremely useful means of sensitizing its members to the ethical and value dimensions of public administration. The Statement itself is viewed as a viable mechanism for communicating shared ethical standards and values to the Institute's members as well as to other public servants and to politicians, journalists, and members of the public. The Statement is a relatively succinct document which, nevertheless, addresses in general terms virtually all the major issues discussed in this book. It has been widely publicized and is used within the Institute as a basis for workshops on ethics and values.

8. Gerald E. Caiden, "Ethics in the Public Service: Codification Misses the Real Target," *Public Personnel Management* 10, no. 1 (1981), p. 149.

9. James S. Bowman, "The Management of Ethics: Codes of Conduct in Organizations," *Public Personnel Management* 10, no. 1 (1981), p. 62.

10. See the review of the empirical evidence on ethical behaviour in private sector corporations in Ronald E. Berenbeim, "An Outbreak of Ethics," *Across the Board* (May 1988), pp. 15-19.

11. See David P. Fauri, "Public Service as Service to Clients," *American Behavioral Scientist* 21 (July/August 1978), pp. 869-70; and *Governing Values* (Ottawa: Supply and Services Canada, 1987).

12. See Kathryn G. Denhardt, *The Ethics of Public Service* (Westport: Greenwood Press, 1988), pp. 144-47.

13. For a discussion of the possibilities of building incentives for responsiveness to clients into the performance evaluation system, see Organization for Economic Cooperation and Development, *Administration as Service* (Paris: OECD Publications, 1986), pp. 106-18; and Perry Moore, "Rewards and Public Employees

Attitudes Toward Client Service," *Public Personnel Management* 6 (March/April 1977), pp. 98-105.

14. See *New York Times*, September 23, 1986; and *CQ Weekly Report* 43 (March 2, 1985), p. 404.

15. *Ottawa Citizen*, March 31, 1987. An extremely detailed analysis of the applicability of the special counsel model to the Canadian system of government is contained in Ontario Law Reform Commission, *Report on Political Activity, Public Comment and Disclosure by Crown Employees* (Toronto: Ministry of the Attorney General, 1986), pp. 327-52.

16. Cooper, *The Responsible Administrator*, p. 126. See also Kenneth Kernaghan, "Evolving Patterns of Administrative Responsiveness to the Public," *International Review of Administrative Sciences* 52 (March 1986), pp. 7-16.

17. *Ethical Conduct in the Public Sector: Report of the Task Force on Conflict of Interest* (Ottawa: Supply and Services Canada, 1984), ch. 13; see also Kenneth Kernaghan, "The Ethics of Public Men," *Policy Options* 6 (June 1985), pp. 31-34.

18. *The Standing Committee of the Legislative Assembly Report on Ministerial Compliance with the Conflict of Interest Guidelines and Recommendations with Respect to Those Guidelines*, Report prepared by John B. Aird for the Ontario Premier, Toronto 1986; and *Commission of Inquiry Into the Facts of Allegations of Conflict of Interest Concerning the Honourable Sinclair M. Stevens* (Ottawa: Supply and Services Canada, 1987), esp. ch. 27.

19. Ibid., p. 348.

Appendix

Statement of Principles Regarding the Conduct of Public Employees

The Institute of Public Administration of Canada

Preamble

The Institute of Public Administration of Canada is committed in its by-laws to promoting and maintaining "high ideals and traditions in the Public Service" and to giving expression "to the considered view of the members on questions of public duty and professional etiquette." To help achieve these objectives, the Institute has, after extensive consultation with its members, adopted this Statement of Principles Regarding the Conduct of Public Employees.

The Institute's dedication to excellence in public service is manifested in large part through efforts to improve the quality of the practice of public administration. We, the members of the Institute, intend that this Statement of Principles should enhance the perform-ance of our members by encouraging high standards of conduct, whether they work in the federal, provincial or local government sectors. We intend also that this Statement should inform the general public, politicians and the news media of the principles and standards which should guide official behaviour.

We believe that high standards of conduct among government officials are central to the maintenance of public trust and confidence in government. We believe also that there is widespread agreement in Canada's public administration community on certain principles and standards of proper conduct. Nevertheless, we recognize that public employees experience conflicts of values or of loyalties. In such cases, the principles in this Statement may provide valuable guidance. We recognize further that on occasion difficult decisions facing public employees can ultimately be resolved only by resorting to individual conscience.

The principles in this Statement are expressed in terms of what should be done as opposed to what shall or must be done. No mechanism is provided for their enforcement. While this Statement is intended for the members of the Institute, we recognize that it can serve as a valuable reference guide for all public employees.

Certain principles in this Statement cannot be easily applied to persons working in such specialized areas of public administration as post-secondary institutions, advisory bodies and public corporations. The environment in which these persons work may dictate a somewhat different approach. For example, the right of faculty members in universities and colleges to academic freedom may be incompatible with limitations on their political rights. Nevertheless, employees in such circumstances are enjoined to adhere to the principles in this Statement that are applicable to them and to the general spirit of the Statement.

The Principles

Accountability

Public employees are accountable for the quality of their advice, for carrying out their assigned duties and for achieving policy and program objectives within the framework of law, prevailing constraints, direction from their superiors, and the limits of the authority and resources at their disposal.

Public employees are accountable on a day-to-day basis to their superiors for their own actions and the actions of their subordinates. They owe their primary duty, however, to their political superiors. They are indirectly accountable to the legislature or council and to the public through their political superiors. Public servants also have a responsibility to report any violation of the law to the appropriate authorities.

Service to the Public

Public employees should provide service to the public in a manner which is courteous, equitable, efficient and effective.

Public employees should be sensitive and responsive to the changing needs, wishes and rights of the public while respecting the legal and constitutional framework within which service to the public is provided.

To promote excellence in public service, public employees have a responsibility to maintain and improve their own competence and to assist in enhancing the competence of their colleagues.

The Public Interest

Public employees should resolve any conflict between their personal or private interests and their official duties in favour of the public interest.

Public employees should seek to serve the public interest by upholding both the letter and the spirit of the laws established by the legislature or council and of the regulations and directions made pursuant to these laws.

Political Neutrality

Public employees should be sensitive to the political process and knowledgeable about the laws and traditions regarding political neutrality that are applicable to their sphere of employment.

It is the responsibility of public employees to provide forthright and objective advice to, and carry out the directions of, their political superiors.

Public employees have a duty to carry out government decisions loyally, irrespective of the party or persons in power and irrespective of their personal opinions.

Political Rights

Public employees should enjoy the fullest possible measure of political rights that is compatible with laws, regulations and conventions designed to preserve the political neutrality of the public service.

Public employees have a responsibility to avoid participation in partisan politics that is likely to impair the political neutrality of the public service or the perception of that neutrality. In return, employees should not be compelled to engage in partisan political activities or be subjected to threats or discrimination for refusing to engage in such activities.

Public employees should not express their personal views on matters of political controversy or on government policy or administration when such comment is likely to impair public confidence in the objective and efficient performance of their duties. It is the responsibility of public employees to seek approval from the appropriate governmental authority whenever they are uncertain as to the legality or propriety of expressing their personal views.

Conflict of Interest

Public employees should not engage in any business or transaction or have any financial or other personal interest that is, or may appear to be, incompatible with the performance of their official duties.

Public employees should not, in the performance of their official duties, seek personal or private gain by granting preferential treatment to any persons.

Public employees should not solicit nor, unless duly authorized, accept transfers of economic value from persons with whom they have contact in their official capacity.

Public employees should not use, or permit the use of, government property of any kind for activities not associated with the performance of their official duties, unless they are authorized to do so.

Public employees should not seek or obtain personal or private gain from the use of information acquired during the course of their official duties which is not generally available to the public.

Confidentiality

Public employees should not disclose to any member of the public, either orally or in writing, any secret or confidential information acquired by virtue of their official position.

Within the bounds of law and propriety, public employees should be sensitive and responsive to the needs of the public, the news media and legislators for information on and explanation of the content and administration of government policies and programs.

Discrimination and Harassment

All public employees have a duty to treat members of the public and one another fairly and to ensure that their work environment is free from discrimination and harassment.

Selected Bibliography

Chapter 1 – Thinking about Responsible Behaviour

Bok, Sissela. *Lying: Moral Choice in Public and Private Life.* New York: Vintage, 1979.

Burke, John P. *Bureaucratic Responsibility.* Baltimore: Johns Hopkins University Press, 1986.

Cooper, Terry L. *The Responsible Administrator.* Port Washington, N.Y.: Kennikat Press, 1982.

Denhardt, Kathryn G. *The Ethics of Public Service.* Westport: Greenwood Press, 1988.

Edwards, Paul, ed. *The Encyclopedia of Philosophy.* New York: Macmillan, 1967.

Fleischman, Joel et al. *Public Duties: The Moral Obligations of Government Officials.* Cambridge: Harvard University Press, 1981.

French, Peter, A. *Ethics in Government.* Englewood Cliffs: Prentice Hall, 1983.

Fried, Charles. *Right and Wrong.* Cambridge: Harvard University Press, 1978.

Hampshire, Stuart et al., eds. *Public and Private Morality.* Cambridge: Cambridge University Press, 1978.

Langford, John W. "Responsibility in the Senior Public Service: Marching to Several Drummers," *Canadian Public Administration* 27 (Winter 1984), pp. 513-21.

Macintyre, Alasdair. *After Virtue,* Notre Dame: University of Notre Dame Press, 1981.

Nagel, Thomas. *The View From Nowhere.* New York: St. Martins, 1983.

Raphael, D.D. *Moral Philosophy.* Oxford: Oxford University Press, 1981.

Rawls, John. *A Theory of Justice.* Cambridge: Harvard University Press, 1971.

Rohr, John A. *Ethics for Bureaucrats.* New York: Marcel Dekker, 2nd ed., 1989.

Scheffler, Samuel. *The Rejection of Consequentialism.* Oxford: Clarendon Press, 1984.

Thompson, Dennis F. *Political Ethics and Public Office.* Cambridge: Harvard University Press, 1987.

Chapter 2 – Acting in the Public Interest

Barry, Brian. *The Liberal Theory of Justice.* Oxford: Clarendon Press, 1973.

Cochran, Clarke E. "Political Science and 'The Public Interest'," *Journal of Politics* 36 (1974), pp. 327-55.

Downs, Anthony. "The Public Interest: Its Meaning in a Democracy." *Social Research* 29 (Spring 1962), pp. 1-36.

Dvorin, Eugene P. and Simmons, Robert H. *From Amoral to Humane Bureaucracy.* San Francisco: Canfield Press, 1972.

Hodgetts, J.E. "Government Responsiveness to the Public Interest: Has Progress Been Made?" *Canadian Public Administration* 24 (Summer 1981), pp. 216-31.

Kernaghan, Kenneth. "The Conscience of the Bureaucrat: Accomplice or Constraint?" *Canadian Pubic Administration* 27 (Winter 1984), pp. 576-91.

Rawls, John. *A Theory of Justice.* Cambridge: Harvard University Press, 1971.

Schubert, Glendon. *The Public Interest: A Critique of a Political Concept.* Glencoe, Ill.: The Free Press, 1960.

Chapter 3 – The Politically Neutral Public Servant

Cassidy, Michael. "Political Rights for Public Servants: A Federal Perspective (1)." *Canadian Public Administration* 29 (Winter 1986), pp. 653-64.

D'Aquino, Thomas. "The Public Service of Canada: The Case for Political Neutrality." *Canadian Public Administration* 27 (Spring 1984), pp. 14-23.

Denton, T.M. "Ministerial Responsibility: A Contemporary Perspective." In R. Schultz et al., eds., *The Canadian Political Process.* Toronto: Holt, Rinehart and Winston, 1979, pp. 344-62.

Forget, Claude E. "L'administration publique: sujet ou objet du pouvoir politique." *Canadian Public Administration* 21 (Summer 1978), pp. 234-42.

Gallant, Edgar. "Political Rights for Public Servants: A Federal Perspective (2)," *Canadian Public Administration* 29 (Winter 1986), pp. 665-68.

Kernaghan, Kenneth. "Changing Concepts of Power and Responsibility in the Canadian Public Service." *Canadian Public Administration* 21 (Fall 1978), pp. 389-406.

Kernaghan, Kenneth. "Political Rights and Political Neutrality: Finding the Balance Point." *Canadian Public Administration* 29 (Winter 1986), pp. 639-52.

Kernaghan, Kenneth. "Politics, Policy and Public Servants: Political Neutrality Revisited." *Canadian Public Administration* 19 (Fall 1976), pp. 432-56.

Kernaghan, Kenneth. "Power, Parliament and Public Servants: Ministerial Responsibility Reexamined." *Canadian Public Policy* 5 (Autumn 1979), pp. 383-96.

MacDonald, Flora. "The Ministers and the Mandarins." *Policy Options* 1 (September-October 1980), pp. 29-31.

Ontario Law Reform Commission. *Political Activity, Public Comment and Disclosure by Crown Employees.* Toronto: Ministry of the Attorney General, 1986.

Osbaldeston, Gordon. "The Public Servant and Politics." *Policy Options* 8 (January 1987), pp. 3-7.

Ostry, Bernard. "Don't Spoil the Public Service." *Policy Options* 8 (January 1987), pp. 7-11.

Robertson, Gordon. "The Deputies' Anonymous Duty." *Policy Options* 4 (July 1983), pp. 11-13.

Segal, Hugh. "The Accountability of Public Servants." *Policy Options* 2 (November/December 1981), pp. 11-12.

Sharp, Mitchell. "The Bureaucratic Elite and Policy Formation." In W.D.K. Kernaghan, ed., *Bureaucracy in Canadian Government.* Toronto: Methuen, 1973, pp. 82-87.

Wilson, V. Seymour. *Canadian Public Policy and Administration.* Toronto: McGraw-Hill Ryerson, 1981, ch. 4.

Chapter 4 – Confidentiality and Privacy

Abel, Elie. *Leaking: Who Does It? Who Benefits? At What Cost?* New York: Priority Press, 1987.

Bok, Sissela. *Secrets: On the Ethics of Concealment and Revelation.* New York: Vintage, 1983.

Ewing, David. *Freedom Inside the Organization.* New York: Dutton, 1977.

Goodin, Robert. *Manipulatory Politics.* New Haven: Yale University Press, 1980.

Ontario Law Reform Commission. *Report on Political Activity, Public Comment and Disclosure by Crown Employees.* Toronto: Ministry of the Attorney General, 1986.

Peters, Charles and Branch, Taylor, eds. *Blowing The Whistle.* New York: Praeger, 1972.

Rachels, James. "Why Privacy Is Important." *Philosophy and Public Affairs* 4 (Summer 1975), pp. 323-332.

Westin, Alan. *Privacy and Freedom.* New York: Atheneum, 1967.

Wilenski, Harold. *Organizational Intelligence: Knowledge and Policy in Government and Industry.* New York: Basic Books, 1967.

Chapter 5 – Service to the Public

Albrecht, Karl and Zemke, Ron. *Service America: Doing Business in the New Economy.* Homewood: Dow Jones-Irwin, 1987.

Canada. *Governing Values.* Ottawa: Supply and Services Canada, 1987.

Frederickson, H. George. *The New Public Administration.* University: The University of Alabama Press, 1980.

Hodgkinson, Christopher. *Towards a Philosophy of Administration.* Oxford: Basil Blackwell, 1978.

Hummel, Ralph P. *The Bureaucratic Experience.* New York: St. Martin's, 1978.

Kranz, H. *The Participatory Bureaucracy.* Lexington: Lexington Books, 1976.

Stewart, John and Clarke, Michael. "The Public Service Orientation: Issues and Dilemmas." *Public Administration* 65 (Summer 1987), pp. 161-77.

Thompson, Victor A. *Without Sympathy or Enthusiasm: The Problem of Administrative Compassion.* University: The University of Alabama Press, 1975.

Wilenski, Peter. *Public Power and Public Administration.* Sydney: Hale and Iremonger, 1986.

Chapter 6 – Conflict of Interest

Association of the Bar of the City of New York. Special Committee on Conflict of Interest Laws. *Conflict of Interest and Federal Service.* Cambridge, Mass.: Harvard University Press, 1960.

Canada. *Ethical Conduct in the Public Sector: Report of the Task Force on Conflict of Interest.* Ottawa: Supply and Services. 1984.

Canada. *Commission of Inquiry into the Facts of Allegations of Conflict of Interest Concerning the Honourable Sinclair M. Stevens (The Parker Commission).* Ottawa: Supply and Services, 1987.

Cranston, Ross F. "Regulating Conflict of Interest of Public Officials: A Comparative Analysis." *Vanderbilt Journal of Transnational Law* 12 (Spring 1979), pp. 215-56.

Kernaghan, Kenneth. "Codes of Ethics and Administrative Responsibility." *Canadian Public Administration* 17 (Winter 1974), pp. 527-41.

Kernaghan, Kenneth. "Codes of Ethics and Public Administration: Progress, Problems and Prospects." *Public Administration (Britain)* 58 (Summer 1980), pp. 207-24.

Kingsley, Jean-Pierre. "Conflict of Interest: A Modern Antidote." *Canadian Public Administration* 29 (Winter 1986), pp. 585-92.

Manning, Bayless. *Federal Conflict of Interest Law.* Cambridge, Mass.: Harvard University Press, 1964.

Taylor, Maureen H. and Filmer, Alan E. "Moonlighting: The Practical Problems." *Canadian Public Administration* 29 (Winter 1986), pp. 592-7.

Williams, Sandra. *Conflict of Interest: The Ethical Dilemma in Politics.* Aldershot, Hants, England: Gower, 1985.

Chapter 7 – The Accountable Public Servant

Canada. Royal Commission on Financial Management and Accountability. *Final Report.* Ottawa: Supply and Services, 1979.

Canada. Privy Council Office. *Responsibility in the Constitution.* Submission to the Royal Commission on Financial Management and Accountability, March 1979.

Cameron, D.M. "Power and Responsibility in the Public Service: Summary of Discussions." *Canadian Public Administration* 21 (Fall 1978), pp. 359-72.

Carman, Robert. "Accountability of Senior Public Servants to Parliament and Its Committees." *Canadian Public Administration* 27 (Winter 1984), pp. 542-55.

Finer, Herman. "Administrative Responsibility in Democratic Government." *Public Administration Review* 1 (Summer 1941), pp. 335-50.

Friedrich, Carl J. "Public Policy and the Nature of Administrative Responsibility." In Carl J. Friedrich and Edward S. Mason, eds., *Public Policy*. Cambridge: Harvard University Press, 1940, pp. 3-24.

Hodgetts, J.E. "Bureaucratic Initiatives, Citizen Involvement, and the Quest for Administrative Accountability." *Transactions of the Royal Society of Canada*. Series IV, Volume 12, 1974.

Hodgetts, J.E. "Implicit Values in the Administration of Public Affairs." *Canadian Public Administration* 25 (Winter 1982), pp. 471-83.

Kernaghan, Kenneth. "Responsible Public Bureaucracy: A Rationale and a Framework for Analysis." *Canadian Public Administration* 16 (Winter 1973), pp. 572-603.

Laframboise, H.L. "Conscience and Conformity: The Uncomfortable Bedfellows of Accountability." *Canadian Public Administration* 26 (Fall 1983), pp. 325-43.

Osbaldeston, Gordon. "How Deputies Are Accountable." *Policy Options* 8 (September 1987), pp. 10-13.

Rosen, Bernard. *Holding Government Bureaucracies Accountable*. New York: Praeger, 1982.

Sutherland, S.L. and Baltacioglu, Y. *Parliamentary Reform and the Federal Public Service*. London: National Centre for Management Research and Development, University of Western Ontario, 1988.

Thompson, Dennis F. "Moral Responsibility of Public Officials: The Problem of Many Hands." *The American Political Science Review* 74 (1980), pp. 905-16.

Chapter 8 – Preserving and Promoting Responsible Behaviour

Bowman, James. "The Management of Ethics: Codes of Conduct in Organizations," *Public Personnel Management* 10 (1981), pp. 59-66.

Caiden, Gerald. "Public Service Ethics: What Should Be Done?" In *Ethics in the Public Service: Comparative Perspectives* (Kenneth Kernaghan and O.P. Dwivedi, eds.) pp. 157-72. Brussels: International Institute of Administrative Sciences, 1983.

Canada, Treasury Board. *Conflict of Interest and Post-Employment Code for the Public Service.* Ottawa: Supply and Services, 1985.

Chapman, Richard. *Ethics in the British Civil Service.* London: Routledge, 1988.

Fleishman, Joel and Payne, Bruce. *Ethical Dilemmas and the Education of Policymakers.* Hastings-on-Hudson: The Hastings Center, 1980.

Hays, Steven W. and Gleissner, Richard R. "Code of Ethics in State Government: A Nationwide Survey." *Public Personnel Management* 10 (1981), pp. 48-58.

Jackson, Michael. "The Eye of Doubt: Neutrality, Responsibility and Morality." *Australian Journal of Public Administration* 46 (September 1987), pp. 280-92.

Kernaghan, Kenneth. *Ethical Conduct: Guidelines for Government Employees.* Toronto: Institute of Public Administration of Canada, 1975.

Langford, John W. "Locking The Revolving Door: A Critique of the Federal Conflict of Interest and Post Employment Code," Discussion Paper, Institute for Research on Public Policy, 1986.

Weller, Steven. "The Effectiveness of Corporate Codes of Ethics." *Journal of Business Ethics* 7 (1988), pp. 389-395.

Related IPAC Publications

Order Address:

The Institute of Public Administration of Canada
L'Institut d'administration publique du Canada
1075 rue Bay St., Suite/Bureau no. 401
Toronto, Ontario, Canada M5S 2B1

Tel. 416-924-8787, Fax 416-924-4992
E-mail: ntl@ipaciapc.ca; web page: www.ipaciapc.ca

Publications on Ethics

*Ethical Conduct: Guidelines for Government Employees /
Comportement professionnel : directives a l'intentions des
fonctionnaires*
by Kenneth Kernaghan

Case Studies

A Conflict of Loyalties
by Kenneth Kernaghan
(Teacher's Manual available)

The Draft Memorandum to Cabinet / Projet de memoire au cabinet
by Douglas G. Hartle

The Alan Jeffrey Affair / L'Affaire Alan Jeffrey
by Kenneth Kernaghan

The Ben Fisher Case
by Nancy LePitre, et al.
(Teacher's Manual available)

The Four Million Dollar Typo: A Case About Accountability
by Laurence E. St. Laurent and Sandford Borins
(Teacher's Manual available)

Perceiving Conflict of Interest: Bureaucratic Discretion in Contracting
by S.L. Sutherland

Related IRPP Publications

Order Address:
The Institute for Research on Public Policy
L'Institut de recherches politiques
1470, rue Peel, Suite 200
Montréal (Québec) H3A 1T1

Peter Aucoin (ed.) — *The Politics and Management of Restraint in Government.* 1981 $17.95

Jacob Finkelman & Shirley B. Goldenberg — *Collective Bargaining in the Public Service: The Federal Experience in Canada.* 2 vols. 1983 $29.95 (set)

Gordon Robertson — *Northern Provinces: A Mistaken Goal.* 1985 $8.00

Nicole Morgan

Implosion: analyse de la croissance de la Fonction publique fédérale canadienne (1945-1985). 1986 $20.00

John W. Langford &
K. Lorne Brownsey (eds.)

The Changing Shape of Government in the Asia-Pacific Region. 1988 $22.00

Timothy W. Plumptre

Beyond the Bottom Line: Management in Government. 1988 $24.95

Tom Kent

Getting Ready for 1999: Ideas for Canada's Politics and Government. 1989 $19.95

Gordon Robertson

A House Divided: Meech Lake, Senate Reform and the Canadian Union. 1989 $14.95

Edward E. Stewart

Cabinet Government in Ontario: A View from Inside. 1989 $14.95

David Zussman &
Jak Jabes

The Vertical Solitude: Managing in the Public Sector. 1989 $24.95